FEDERAL BUDGETING
THE CHOICE OF GOVERNMENT PROGRAMS

By

MURRAY L. WEIDENBAUM

PUBLISHED AND DISTRIBUTED BY THE

AMERICAN ENTERPRISE INSTITUTE

FOR PUBLIC POLICY RESEARCH

WASHINGTON, D.C.

February 1964

Dr. Weidenbaum, senior economist at the Stanford Research Institute, was formerly an economist with the Federal Bureau of the Budget and has served as adviser to other government agencies. Also, he has been an economist with the Boeing Company and has worked extensively in the fields of governmental administration, budgeting, and expenditure as well as defense economics.

Price: $1.00

AMERICAN ENTERPRISE INSTITUTE
For Public Policy Research

THE AMERICAN ENTERPRISE INSTITUTE FOR PUBLIC POLICY RESEARCH, established in 1943, is a nonpartisan research and educational organization which studies national policy problems.

Institute publications take two major forms:

1. LEGISLATIVE AND SPECIAL ANALYSES—factual analyses of current legislative proposals and other public policy issues before the Congress prepared with the help of recognized experts in the academic world and in the fields of law and government. A typical analysis features: (1) pertinent background, (2) a digest of significant elements, and (3) a discussion, pro and con, of the issues. The reports reflect no policy position in favor of or against specific proposals.

2. LONG-RANGE STUDIES—basic studies of major national problems of significance for public policy. The Institute, with the counsel of its Advisory Board, utilizes the services of competent scholars, but the opinions expressed are those of the authors and represent no policy position on the part of the Institute.

ADVISORY BOARD

CONTENTS

FEDERAL BUDGETING
THE CHOICE OF GOVERNMENT PROGRAMS

INTRODUCTION

The Budget, Strange Fish and Monster Vast
To Which from All Sides the Hook is Cast.
                                        —Victor Hugo

IN THE OFFICE of one former director of the Bureau of the Budget, there once hung a chart entitled, "The Tools of Budgeting." Three such tools were portrayed—crystal ball, some dice, and a pair of scissors.

It well may be that these items still represent the most realistic techniques for preparing and reviewing budgetary recommendations. Nevertheless, this study attempts to supply more formal methodology to the process.

Essentially, the purpose is to demonstrate how some relatively simple economic concepts can be applied toward the achievement of improved allocations of government funds among alternative uses. It is hoped that the central problem of budgeting will thus be highlighted; namely, the choice of government programs.

This study of Federal Government spending is based on the belief that—despite all of the well-intentioned attempts to reduce budgeted expenditures or otherwise reform or modify the presidential budgetary recommendations—many of the efforts are unsuccessful for one or both of the following reasons:

1. Lack of a proper public understanding as to how the budgetary system works in practice, particularly with respect to the mechanism for funding government programs and the methods of review and control which it offers, and

2. Lack on the part of the Congress of effective budget-reviewing tools and mechanisms to assist it toward wise decisions in the determination of the amounts of public funds that should be expended and in the allocation of these funds among the various government programs.

For the purpose of appraising means for overcoming these obstacles, this study first offers an explanation of the pressures for instituting, maintaining, and expanding government spending programs. It is demonstrated that the usual situation is for any given government spending program to have a specific group of supporters who think they benefit more from the government expenditure than they would from the general tax reduction which might be permitted by the elimination of the program.

The next section describes the sequences of the government spending process, particularly highlighting the key points of control, some of which are not generally considered to be parts of the budgetary process itself. These latter control points include the enactment by the Congress of basic legislation authorizing government programs to be carried on and the apportionment and allotment of funds by Executive Branch officials.

Subsequently, by way of a case study, a detailed analysis is undertaken of the 1964 budget prepared by the President. This review shows the substantial limitations that exist as to the proportion of the federal budget which may be subjected to effective congressional review and control each year through the appropriating process. For example, the bulk of the civilian welfare expenditures is relatively immune from this budgetary scrutiny.

This material is followed by attempts to indicate several lines of potential improvement in both the preparation of the federal budget in the Executive Branch and the review of the budget by the Congress.

A framework is suggested for preparation of the federal budget which would permit greater choice among the various alternative government programs and a more deliberate and systematic allocation of budget funds among the major purposes of government. Finally, a format is presented of a means of enabling the Congress to relate actions on individual bills and appropriation items to the total budget.

It is hoped that this study will be of value to students of budgeting. To the economy minded, this study describes the problems involved in "cutting" the budget, indicating the more promising approaches and hopefully suggesting certain newer and more effective tools.

For those more concerned with fiscal and economic policy, this study brings to light numerous built-in rigidities in the composition of government spending which inhibit the exercise of discretion in the relating of budget decisions to more general economic or fiscal policy objectives.

To all of these and other groups, this study attempts, by suggesting several approaches, to show the desirability of and need for more effective methods of federal budgeting and programming.

THE PRESSURES FOR
GOVERNMENT SPENDING

A STUDY FOCUSED on methods of improving controls over governmental spending necessarily begins with an analysis of the motivations and the pressures that cause the Federal Government to undertake its great variety of activities. These pressures need to be borne in mind in connection with succeeding sections which describe the formal government budgetary process and its built-in rigidities. Official budgetary statistics will be drawn upon, but they will be supplemented by other information.

Fundamentally, the purpose of this section is to show more

4

clearly the following basic relevant relationships:

Recipients of federal expenditures are very highly concentrated in specific segments of the population. This holds whether the category of analysis used is type of expenditure, location of the activity, or the industries and groups which are benefited.

Consequently, the common and usual situation is for any given government expenditure program to have a specific clientele whose members are benefited more directly—or at least so they think—from the particular government expenditure program than they would be from the relatively modest general tax reduction which might be permitted by the elimination of the program.

These bodies of beneficiaries of expenditure programs are motivated to become special pleaders, often on an organized basis, for the continuance and expansion of the programs in which they are interested.

The impact of the aggressive and pinpointed support of the many programs tends to outweigh, in the absence of the rare "taxpayers' uprising," any diffused and usually unspoken opposition that may be harbored by the general taxpaying public.

In contrast, if the unrealistic situation were to prevail wherein the direct benefits from each type of government spending were divided equally among all persons, then the average citizen might consider himself equally benefited either by a continuation of spending for a given set of government programs or by a general tax reduction resulting from elimination of such programs. Under this circumstance, he would be likely to judge the desirability of private vs. public spending, in the decision area under consideration, solely from the viewpoint of the national interest.

Different types of pressures generated in support of the varied federal expenditure programs are outlined in the expenditure analyses that follow. In the presentation of these analyses, however, there is no intent to imply that self-interest pressures generally preclude or necessarily dominate considerations of the national interest in the reaching of decisions on federal expenditure programs.

5

Concentration of Expenditures by Function

Opportunities that exist for the build-up of federal expenditure pressures from various segments of the population are readily discernible from simple analyses of the federal budget in terms of agencies by which and functions for which the budgeted funds are expended.

By way of example, Table 1 shows the distribution of federal expenditures for the 1964 fiscal year, as estimated in the budget document when submitted to the Congress, according to the department or agency to which funds are appropriated. It is apparent that a handful of agencies—particularly the Defense, Treasury, Agriculture, and Health-Education-Welfare departments—account for the great bulk of the spending. The aggregate expenditures of these four departments were estimated to represent 73 percent of the total for the year. As demonstrated subsequently, the three civilian departmental budgets contain

Table 1
ESTIMATED FEDERAL EXPENDITURES
BY AGENCY
Fiscal Year 1964
(millions of dollars)

Agency	Administrative budget	Trust funds
Department of Defense	$52,140	$ 32
Treasury Department	11,232	22
Department of Agriculture	6,565	48
Department of Health, Education, and Welfare	5,742	16,650
Veterans Administration	5,470	548
Funds appropriated to the President [1]	4,375	574
National Aeronautics and Space Administration	4,200	
Atomic Energy Commission	2,850	
Department of the Interior	1,165	84
Department of Commerce	895	3,401
Department of Labor	433	3,770
Civil Service Commission	112	1,275
Railroad Retirement Board	12	1,099
All other	3,611	879
Total	$98,802[2]	$28,382[2]

[1] Mainly foreign aid.
[2] Totals include $4,707 million in intragovernmental transactions and adjustments.
Source: *The Budget of the United States Government for the Fiscal Year Ending June 30, 1964* (Washington: U. S. Government Printing Office, 1963), pp. 41 ff.

Table 2
FEDERAL GOVERNMENT PAYMENTS TO THE PUBLIC
Fiscal Year 1964

Function	Amount (millions)	Percent
National defense	$56,006	45.7
Health, labor, and welfare	27,424	22.4
Interest	7,723	6.3
Commerce and transportation	6,677	5.5
Veterans benefits and services	5,978	4.9
Agriculture	5,764	4.7
Space research and technology	4,200	3.4
International affairs and finance	2,743	2.2
Natural resources	2,596	2.1
General government	2,197	1.8
Education	1,495	1.2
Housing and community development	1,124	.9
Undistributed adjustments [1]	−1,451	−1.1
Total	$122,477	100.0

[1] Intragovernmental payments that cannot be allocated by functions, such as payments to federal employees' retirement funds. The remainder of the $4,707 of intragovernmental transactions and adjustments (shown in Table 1) has been deducted from individual items.

Source: *The Budget of the United States Government for the Fiscal Year Ending June 30, 1964* (Washington: U. S. Government Printing Office, 1963), p. 430.

large amounts of rigidly established items that are relatively uncontrollable through the appropriating process.

The activities of a number of the agencies included in the "All other" category of Table 1 may have important effects on the nation, but they do not involve large flows of expenditure. The "All other" group includes the Justice, Post Office, and State departments, Legislative Branch, Judiciary, Office of the President and various regulatory commissions, and other independent agencies.

The second of the two standard official classifications of Federal Government spending is in terms of the function, or purpose, for which the disbursements are made. This is presented in Table 2, which also consolidates the administrative budget and trust fund expenditures[1] reported separately in Table 1, elim-

---

[1] The administrative budget covers only funds which are considered to be "government-owned," while trust funds are established to account for funds which are received, held, and expended in a "fiduciary" capacity by the government in carrying out specific purposes and programs. Some of the so-called trust funds involve a questionable fiduciary relationship, particularly as compared to private funds. Cf. Appendix A, p. 86.

inating $4,707 million in intragovernmental transactions and adjustments between the administrative budget and trust funds.

The concentration of federal expenditures in a few program areas is even more apparent in the functional breakdown than was revealed by the distribution of federal expenditures by agency. Two functions—national defense and health-labor-welfare—alone account for 68 percent of the total federal payments to the public.

With the single exception of interest on the public debt, each of the functional categories of estimated expenditures listed in Table 2 has its own clientele of individuals, groups, or other entities that have direct interests in the expenditures and are capable of petitioning for and otherwise seeking to secure the continuance and expansion of the expenditures.

Partial lists of these affected groups, far from complete, are presented here for illustrative purposes:

National Defense: (1) Military personnel, both from the standpoint of their belief in a strong national defense establishment and from the viewpoint of their personal stake in these programs; (2) business and industrial establishments holding defense contracts and subcontracts, and their employees; (3) public and private institutions holding research contracts or receiving research grants, and their personnel.

Health, Labor, and Welfare: (1) The aged, and other recipients and prospective recipients of Old Age, Survivors, and Disability Insurance benefits; (2) persons with pension rights under Civil Service and railroad retirement systems; (3) labor organizations and individual employees with interests in unemployment and related benefits; (4) recipients of public assistance and their families.

Commerce and Transportation: (1) Highway users; (2) highway construction contractors and their employees; (3) commercial aviation and maritime interests receiving federal aid; (4) communities and business concerns receiving Area Redevelopment Administration loans and grants; (5) beneficiaries of Small Business Administration loans.

Veterans Benefits and Services: War veterans and their families.

Agriculture: (1) Farmers; (2) users of Rural Electrification Administration services; (3) rural residents, not necessarily farmers, utilizing credit and related services of the Agriculture Department.

Space Research and Technology: (1) Holders of NASA contracts and their employees; (2) associated scientists.

International Affairs and Finance: Domestic producers of goods and agricultural commodities disposed of through operation of economic aid programs. (Foreign military aid is included under National Defense.)

Natural Resources: (1) Beneficiaries of reclamation and other types of public works projects; (2) sportsmen; (3) conservationists.

General Government: Federal employees (who as a class also have an interest in all other functional categories of federal expenditures).

Education: (1) Colleges and universities benefiting from loans, grants, and research contracts; (2) members of the educational profession and others with particular interests in programs of federal aid for elementary and secondary schools.

Housing and Community Development: Individuals, business concerns, and local governmental units benefiting directly from public housing, urban renewal, and community facility loans and grants.

The above listing illustrates the pattern of the build-up of pressures behind specific expenditure programs.

Regional Concentrations of Federal Expenditures

Certain types of federal expenditures, by their nature, tend toward heavy concentrations in limited numbers of geographical areas. This is true, for example, of expenditures for industrially produced commodities purchased by the Federal Government. Another example is offered by pay and other expenditures that accompany concentrations of military installations and of civilian employees of the government. Similarly, varied types of grants-in-aid, subsidies, and health-labor-welfare payments tend toward regional concentrations, although to a lesser degree.

It follows that where there are concentrations of the expenditures, there also will be concentrations of the "clientele" of the various kinds of federal payments to the public. The result is localization of the pressures for continuance and expansion of federal spending programs.

The extent to which there have developed concentrations of federal expenditures in geographical regions is suggested by estimates prepared recently, by the Legislative Reference Service of the Library of Congress, of the distribution of 1959-61 federal expenditures by resident states of recipients. The word, "suggested," is used because the Library of Congress analysis of state-wide areas necessarily does not deal with the further locali-

Table 3

DISTRIBUTION OF FEDERAL EXPENDITURES BY STATE AVERAGE
PER CAPITA AMOUNTS FOR
FISCAL YEARS 1959-61

State	Per capita average annual amount	Indices	
		Per capita relative to U. S. average (U. S. average = 100)	Amount per $1,000 of personal income relative to U. S. average (U. S. average = 100)
Alaska	$2,629	577	478
District of Columbia	1,547	339	251
Hawaii	1,087	238	241
Maryland	738	162	150
Virginia	705	154	186
Washington	702	154	148
California	639	140	114
Kansas	618	136	145
Rhode Island	617	135	135
Nevada	609	134	106
Wyoming	607	133	128
New Mexico	606	133	161
Massachusetts	594	130	115
Colorado	567	124	120
New Hampshire	556	122	132
Connecticut	540	118	92
Montana	507	111	120
Maine	505	111	131
Arizona	495	109	121
New Jersey	488	107	89
Delaware	484	106	78
Utah	479	105	121
Oklahoma	476	104	125
South Dakota	469	103	133
Texas	454	100	114

State	Per capita average annual amount	Indices	
		Per capita relative to U. S. average (U. S. average = 100)	Amount per $1,000 of personal income relative to U. S. average (U. S. average = 100)
New York	$448	98	78
Florida	446	98	109
Nebraska	435	95	101
Georgia	416	91	127
Illinois	412	90	76
Missouri	412	90	91
North Dakota	406	89	117
South Carolina	403	88	142
Kentucky	392	86	122
Idaho	387	85	103
Alabama	378	83	126
Ohio	370	81	77
Vermont	361	79	95
Pennsylvania	360	79	77
Indiana	351	77	79
Oregon	346	76	75
North Carolina	336	74	106
Mississippi	327	72	136
Arkansas	321	70	117
Louisiana	315	69	94
Iowa	307	67	73
Michigan	306	67	65
Minnesota	304	67	72
Tennessee	302	66	95
Wisconsin	302	66	68
West Virginia	281	62	81

Source: I. M. Labovitz, *Federal Revenues and Expenditures in the Several States, Averages for the Fiscal Years 1959-61* (Washington: Library of Congress, September 19, 1962), pp. 12-15.

zation of concentrations of federal expenditures within the states.

Data based on the Library of Congress estimates are presented in Table 3. In preparing the original estimates, it was found that in the case of such programs as grants to states, social security payments, veterans pensions, and salaries of government employees, the location of the recipient is quite clear. For such items as defense procurement expenditures, the state-by-state distribution was made on the basis of estimates of the location of the employment on defense work. In these and other estimating techniques that were followed, the Library of Congress study is believed to be the most objective analysis of its kind that is available.

In Table 3, the 50 states and the District of Columbia are ranked according to their disproportionate shares of federal expenditures. For example, Texas is shown in the middle of the table with an index number of 100. This signifies that the federal expenditures which were made in or allocable to Texas amounted on a per capita basis to exactly the nation-wide per capita average of the expenditures—that is, to exactly the same amount as if all federal spending were allocated evenly according to population.

In contrast, the expenditures in Alaska were 5.77 times the amount that would have accrued on a nation-wide, even per capita, basis; in Virginia and Washington, they were 54 percent greater. At the other end of the distribution, West Virginia received only 62 percent of the amount that would have obtained on a straight per capita distribution. (It should be borne in mind that these data cover only the fiscal years 1959-61. Presumably, other periods would yield some variations in the individual estimates.)

A related question is the extent to which federal expenditures may be distributed more in accordance with the current wealth of a state (as measured by the flow of personal income) and, hence in some way, in accordance with the taxpaying capability. Table 3 also shows, pertaining to this question, the great variance among states of federal expenditures per each $1,000 of personal income received in the state.

Still another way of looking at the matter of geographical concentrations of federal expenditures is to consider the importance of such expenditures to each state's economy. Figure 1 represents an attempt to do this for defense purchases, which account for approximately 90 percent of federal contracts awarded each year. The 12 states shown with shadings are those in which the direct employment in major defense industries accounts for 10 percent or more of each state's total industrial employment.

In the case of seven states—Kansas, California, Washington, New Mexico, Connecticut, Arizona, and Utah—defense work accounts for 20 to 30 percent of the total manufacturing employment. The Figure is based on data for the aircraft, ordnance, shipbuilding, electronics, and communications industries as representative of defense work. Other portions of the economy, such as steel and metal fabricators, provide supplies and equipment to

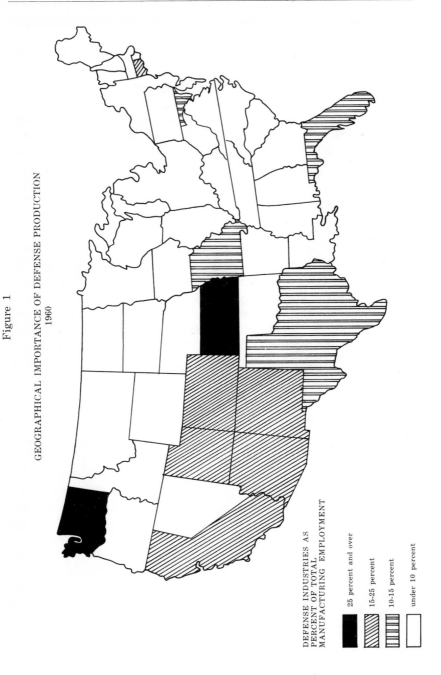

Figure 1

GEOGRAPHICAL IMPORTANCE OF DEFENSE PRODUCTION
1960

DEFENSE INDUSTRIES AS
PERCENT OF TOTAL
MANUFACTURING EMPLOYMENT

25 percent and over

15-25 percent

10-15 percent

under 10 percent

these major defense producers, but are not so heavily dependent on defense production for their sales.

Other states, such as New York, Illinois, and Pennsylvania have absolutely large concentrations of defense industry. However, because of the relative size of their total industrial bases, these latter states do not depend as heavily on defense work as the states designated in Figure 1. In recent years, a number of industrial states have launched intensified efforts to increase their shares of defense production,[2] another indication of the pressures resulting from the uneven distribution of federal expenditures.

Concentration by Industry

Most purchases which the Federal Government makes from private industry are extremely specialized. As revealed by Table 4, more than nine-tenths of the contracts awarded by the Federal Government last year were for military and space equipment. The orders for missiles alone exceeded the purchases of all the civilian departments. In fact, their totals were almost three times the dollar value of orders placed by these other agencies.

It thus becomes apparent that the bulk of federal purchases centers on the output of special types of industrial producers of heavy equipment—aircraft, missiles, electronics, ships, and ordnance. This is not to imply that there is anything insidious in such an industrial concentration. Given the current status of international tensions, the strength of the Communist threat, and the new concepts in military hardware made available through advancing technology, it is to be expected that the bulk of the defense orders should go to industries which have the capability to produce the relatively unique weapon systems and space equipment required for the national security.[3]

---

[2] See, for example, the discussion in the Senate on the Department of Defense Appropriation Bill for the fiscal year 1964, *Congressional Record,* September 24, 1963, pp. 16948-52.

[3] Cf. M. L. Weidenbaum, "The Impact of Military Procurement on American Industry," in J. A. Stockfisch, editor, *Planning and Forecasting in the Defense Industries* (Belmont, Calif.: Wadsworth Publishing Co., 1962), pp. 135-74.

Table 4
CONTRACTS AWARDED BY THE FEDERAL GOVERNMENT
Fiscal Year 1962

	Amount (in millions)	Percent
National Security		
Missiles	$6,690	22.6
Aircraft	5,105	17.3
Electronics systems	3,306	11.2
Ordnance and weapons	2,185	7.4
Ships	1,475	5.0
Construction	1,214	4.1
Space (NASA)	1,054	3.6
All other military	6,173	20.9
Subtotal	$27,201	92.1
Civilian		
General Services Administration [1]	901	3.1
Department of the Interior	328	1.1
Tennessee Valley Authority	214	.7
Department of Commerce	198	.7
All other [2]	718	2.3
Subtotal	$ 2,359	7.9
Total	$29,560	100.0

[1] Includes orders placed by other agencies under indefinite quantity contracts awarded by G.S.A.

[2] Excludes the Atomic Energy Commission, much of whose procurement consists of cost-reimbursed agreements for operation and construction of large-scale facilities.

Source: U. S. Department of Defense, *Military Prime Contracts Awards and Subcontract Payments, July 1961-June 1962*, September 27, 1962, p. 20; U. S. Senate, Select Committee on Small Business, *The Role of Small Business in Government Procurement, 1962-1963*, 1962, pp. 38-39.

Nevertheless, this concentration does mean that the employees of these major government contractors, and the other companies supplying goods and services to the prime contractors as well as to their employees, have become dependent in large measure on government work. Figure 1 illustrates, in part, the resultant geographic distribution of this important economic impact.

Finally, the extent to which some individual industries have come to regard the Federal Government as a major customer may be observed through an examination of the data in Table 5. Here are listed 24 industries for which, according to the latest available Census of Manufactures, the government represents at least one-twentieth of the total market. In several cases, over half of the total sales of an entire industry are made directly to the government.

For individual firms in these industries, the government may represent a far more important source of business than indicated by industry averages. Also the relative importance of the Federal Government as a customer is understated by these data. The table is limited to sales made directly by the manufacturer to the government and does not take account of the portion of the output of these, and other industries, which are purchased by the government through retailers, wholesalers, and other "middlemen."

Some Observations

The preceding analysis has attempted to point out the extent to which individual regions, industries, and groups have become

Table 5

INDUSTRIES FOR WHICH THE FEDERAL GOVERNMENT IS AN
IMPORTANT CUSTOMER

Industry	Shipments to Federal Government as percent of total
Complete aircraft	95
Aircraft propellers	75
Engines for aircraft and missiles	54
Shipbuilding and repair	39
Scientific instruments	38
Rice mill products	30
Radio and TV equipment	27
Electrical measuring instruments	15
Trucks and trailers	10
Optical instruments	9
Primary batteries	9
Electronic tubes	8
Photographic equipment	8
Computing machines	7
Internal combustion engines	6
Machine tools	6
Storage batteries	6
Appliance wire and cord	6
Envelopes	6
Misc. general industry machinery	5
Mechanical measuring instruments	5
Wiring devices and supplies	5
Boatbuilding and repair	5
Truck and bus bodies	5

Source: *1958 Census of Manufactures* (latest year available).

attached to or dependent upon specific categories of federal expenditures.[4] These attachments and dependencies may go a long way towards explaining why most effective attempts to reduce requested amounts of federal spending authority have focused on new and proposed programs that have not yet gained a niche in the fabric of society. In any event, it points up the difficulties involved in making major changes in the existing composition and resultant distribution of federal operations and disbursements. This problem is analyzed further, from a different approach, in the next section.

---

[4] Cf. "One of the basic problems of federal finance is the power exercised by organized interest and section groups. . . . Once the federal government embarks on a program of federal aid it is unlikely that it can ever stop or curtail it in the face of these pressures." Joseph P. Harris, "Needed Reforms in the Federal Budget System," *Public Administration Review*, Autumn 1952, pp. 243-44.

FEDERAL SPENDING AND
THE LOCALITY

IN CONTRAST to the theme and aggregate approach of the preceding section, this section focuses on a single city to examine the array of governmental activities and funds that are or can be available at the local level. The purpose of this examination is to provide further insight into the character of local pressures which may be generated in support of given federal expenditure programs.

Obviously, a great many cities and towns in the United States contain local representatives of various "old-line" federal departments, bureaus, and agencies, such as the FBI and the Bureau of Labor Statistics. The established operating activities thus represented generally function with only mild efforts to expand in pace with normal population and workload growth.

However, there also are a great many federal programs of a "developmental" character which often are the objects of aggressive local efforts to promote their expansion. There are the programs relating to airports, flood control projects, post office buildings, highways, health research, and similar "investment" type projects for which local communities vie for selection.

The Atlanta, Georgia, metropolitan area presents an interesting case, not because of its uniqueness but because of its typical position as a recipient of and beneficiary from federal programs and activities. It is singled out in this study only because the information is available as the result of a special report by the U. S. Housing and Home Finance Agency.[1] The HHFA lists 33 different federal "developmental" programs, of wide variety, in the Atlanta metropolitan area. The funds authorized for these programs in 1962, including grants as well as direct expenditures and loans as well as loan guarantees, totaled $117,698,000.

Grants and Matching Funds

The Department of Commerce, the Department of Health, Education, and Welfare, the Housing and Home Finance Agency, and the Federal Aviation Agency each provided one or more types of grants and matching funds to the Atlanta area in 1962. These varied from secondary road construction ($5,000) to air pollution research ($35,000). The $35,841,000 in grants to Atlanta could be categorized as follows:

Transportation facilities—primary roads, secondary roads, urban roads, interstate highway, airport construction.

Education—payments to school districts.

Health—hospital construction, waste treatment works, air pollution research, water pollution research, health facility and construction.

Urban facilities—urban renewal, urban planning.

---

[1] Testimony of Robert C. Weaver, Administrator, Housing and Home Finance Agency in U. S. Senate, Committee on Government Operations, *Role of the Federal Government in Metropolitan Areas* (Washington: U. S. Government Printing Office, 1963), pp. 82-83.

Direct Federal Expenditures

In addition to the above grants-in-aid, the Veterans Administration and the Departments of Agriculture, Defense, and Interior each conducted several developmental activities in Atlanta in 1962. These programs were mainly in various fields of natural resource development. The following is a classification of these various direct federal expenditure programs, which totaled $2,296,000 in 1962:

> *Natural resource development*—Altoona Dam recreation facilities, Buford Dam construction, flood prevention, watershed investigation, construction of park facilities, rehabilitation of park facilities, investigation of fish and wildlife, saline water research.

Health—veterans hospital alterations.

Agriculture—farm research.

Defense—construction of reserve, national guard, and other facilities.

Loans and Advances

Loans to individuals, business firms, and local governments in the Atlanta area were also made or planned for in 1962 by the Department of Agriculture, the Housing and Home Finance Agency, the Small Business Administration, and the Veterans Administration. These credit operations (totaling $594,000) came within the following categories:

> *Urban facilities*—direct housing loans, advances for public works planning.

Agriculture—farm loans, rural housing loans.

Business—loans to small business.

Insuring and Leaseback Programs

Finally, three different agencies provided loan insurance and guarantees to the Atlanta area in 1962—the Department of Agriculture, the Veterans Administration, and the Housing and Home Finance Agency. One agency—the Post Office Department

—entered into "leaseback" agreements with private companies for the construction of post offices.

The loan insurance and guarantee programs do not involve any federal expenditure, other than for administration, except in the event of default. Under the "leaseback" program, the Post Office obtains the use of a building constructed to its specifications and makes payments on a lease over an extended period of time rather than paying the full cost of the facility in cash at the outset.

The Federal Government insured or entered into leaseback agreements in Atlanta in 1962 aggregating $78,966,000. The programs may be classified as follows:

> *Urban facilities*—insured housing loans, public housing construction, guaranteed veterans housing loans.
>
> *Agriculture*—insured farm ownership loans.
>
> *Government operations*—post office building leaseback.

Comments

The above description of federal developmental programs in the Atlanta metropolitan area in 1962 shows the great variety of government projects in a single city in a single year. This sample of federal projects yielded programs covering transportation, education, health, urban development, agriculture, and business, as well as defense and government operations.

The federal agencies involved were the Departments of Agriculture, Commerce, Defense, Health, Education, and Welfare, and Post Office, the Federal Aviation Agency, the Housing and Home Finance Agency, the Small Business Administration, and the Veterans Administration.

The financial methods used include grants and matching funds, direct federal expenditures, loan and advance loan programs, and insuring and leaseback programs.

Although the remainder of this study is devoted to the analyzing of federal programs and expenditures from a national viewpoint, it is helpful to keep in mind the significance of the impact of these programs—and the resultant pressures for their

21

continuation and expansion—at the local level. From the viewpoint of many in the locality, who often rationalize that the government money will be spent anyway, the overriding issue usually is that of whether the locality will obtain its "fair" share. The argument is often voiced that if city "A" turns down the opportunity to obtain a grant from agency "X," the money will go to city "B"—but the relative amounts of federal taxes paid by the people living in A and B will remain unaffected.

THE MECHANICS OF
GOVERNMENT SPENDING

ESSENTIAL TO THE ANALYZING of federal budgetary control problems is an understanding of the mechanics of the spending processes. It is commonly thought that Congress simply enacts appropriations and that the Federal Government agencies then spend the money. In fact, even quite knowledgeable economists sometime short-circuit the process in their descriptions and state that the Congress "legislates government expenditures."

In practice, the process through which Federal Government expenditures are made is a lengthy and intricate one. An attempt is made here to explain the major steps in such detail as may be pertinent to the subject of budgetary control.[1]

Basic Authorizing Legislation

The first step toward establishment of the nature and amount of Federal Government expenditures is not the enactment of appropriations but the making of decisions on the functions which the government should perform. This step normally takes the form of enactment by the Congress of basic legislation creating a given agency, program, or activity and authorizing the appropriation of funds therefore. Some statute, such as the permanent authorization for the Council of Economic Advisers or the annual authorization for the foreign aid program, must be on the books before an appropriation can be enacted to provide funds for the agency or program involved.

Authorizations for limited periods, of course, assure a subsequent legislative review before the program is continued beyond the initial period. For example, the national defense education program, enacted in 1961, was scheduled to expire in 1963 unless extended by additional substantive legislation.[2]

This is the result of congressional procedure rather than statutory requirement. The House rule provides that "no appropriation shall be reported in any general appropriation bill, or be in order as an amendment thereto, for any expenditures not previously authorized by law. . . ."[3] The Senate rule is generally similar.

There are a number of exceptions. For example, the operations of the military establishment have been sanctioned by the Constitution and no general authorizing legislation is necessary; only appropriations enacted by the Congress are needed to enable it to spend government money (except for capital outlays and research and development which do require separate authorizations).

---

[1] A more detailed exposition is contained in M. L. Weidenbaum, "The Economic Impact of the Government Spending Process," *The Business Review*, The University of Houston, Vol. 8, Spring 1961, pp. 3-47.

[2] Public Law 344, 87th Congress, 1st Session, signed October 3, 1961.

[3] *Constitution, Jefferson's Manual and Rules of the House of Representatives*, House Document No. 766, 80th Congress, 2d Session (Washington: U. S. Government Printing Office, 1949), rule 21, clause 2.

In general, authorizing legislation is enacted before funds are granted, and the financial aspects of a government activity are considered separately by the Congress. However, some basic authorizing statutes do simultaneously grant federal agencies financial authority of various types. The Federal-Aid Highway Act, for example, both authorizes the program of aid to the states and enables the Bureau of Public Roads to commit the Federal Government to make specific grants for highway construction.[4] Under this circumstance, the annual appropriation request is for the purpose of "liquidating" the obligations previously incurred and is a mere formality.

In common parlance, this procedure is often referred to as "backdoor spending." Technically, it is backdoor authorization of spending, since the expenditures are made in the same fashion as expenditures out of appropriations and like them, are included in the respective budget totals. As is demonstrated in succeeding sections of this study, however, such "backdoor authorizations" of government spending bypass the detailed review of appropriations committees of both the House of Representatives and the Senate.

Many government corporations and other business-type enterprises, particularly those operating lending programs, are authorized by basic legislation to spend the receipts from their operations without securing annual appropriations from the Congress.[5]

In any budgetary control efforts, consideration must be given to the increment of basic authorizing legislation which is proposed each year—the enactment of new substantive legislation, the extension of expiring legislation, and the modification or repeal of existing statutes—for here is the birth stage, and rebirth and growth stages, of a substantial proportion of federal spending.

This is the stage where the basic policy decisions are made. The kind of farm program, the types of public assistance payments, the level of highway grants are all decided at this stage. However, since the substantive committees of the Congress

---

[4] Public Law 627, 84th Congress.
[5] Budget and Accounting Act of 1921 (U.S.C. 11-16); Budget and Accounting Procedures Act of 1950 (Public Law 784, 81st Congress).

which handle enabling or authorizing legislation (e.g., Judiciary or Foreign Relations or Public Works), rather than the appropriations committees, function during this phase, cost impacts of the new programs ordinarily are relegated to secondary consideration.

The individual substantive committees of the Congress, as they consider legislation with large expenditure significance, usually do not have the opportunity to balance one program against another or to take account of the taxes needed to finance them.[6] The dominant pressure on the legislative or substantive committee ordinarily comes from those favoring a particular program. Prospective beneficiaries, as has been pointed out earlier, are not as concerned with questions of cost as the general taxpayer who advocates economy.

It should be noted that the congressional prohibition on appropriations in the absence of previously enacted authorizing legislation often is a one-way street. In numerous cases, such as the highway program previously mentioned, substantive legislation contains the funding authority which directly—often rigidly—determines the amount of the appropriation that may be enacted.

The reader may sympathize with Dr. Colm's lament concerning the lack of coordination between enabling legislation and appropriations:

> It is a cause for endless bewilderment and wasted effort that enabling legislation often not only establishes the basic purpose of an activity, but also authorizes a specific amount for a specific year.[7]

Requests for New Funds

Each spring, the Bureau of the Budget (a unit in the Executive Office of the President) begins planning the budget for the following fiscal year. With information from each major government department and agency, and subsequent staff work, the

---

[6] "The committees which pass upon authorizations for new or expanded programs have little or no feeling of responsibility for the financial condition of the government. They are primarily interested, as a rule, in advancing the particular program." Harris, *op. cit.*, p. 244.

[7] Gerhard Colm, with the the assistance of Marilyn Young, *The Federal Budget and the National Economy*, National Planning Association, March 1955, p. 30.

President makes an initial determination of the budget level for each major agency. Merely an initial decision at this stage, it will be subject to change at numerous subsequent points in the process.

On the basis of the initial target figures, each department begins detailed preparation of budget submissions. These budgets are not prepared from a clean slate, but take account of the program and expenditure commitments arising from the variety of authorizing legislation which is on the books. Budget preparation generally lasts through the summer and early fall. In the late fall, the Budget Bureau conducts a detailed review of the agency submissions. The outcome goes to the President for his review and then incorporation into the executive budget document.

In January of each year the President transmits to the Congress the budget for the coming fiscal year, the 12-month period beginning the following July 1. In addition to much supporting and historical data, the budget contains the President's estimates of the Federal Government's need for new appropriations and other funding (the various types are described below) for the coming fiscal year. In the case of proposed programs, the President recommends both the needed legislative authority and the necessary "supplemental" appropriation requests which, contingent upon passage of the authorizing legislation, will be sent to the Congress after the consideration of the regular appropriation bills.

From time to time exigencies arise not covered in the budget (such as greater than expected applications for public assistance) which require the President to make further appropriation requests to the Congress. For example, the enactment of legislation with funding requirements not included in the budget or unanticipated U. S. commitments in international conflicts have resulted in such supplemental requests.

Congressional Enactment of Appropriations

The Constitution provides that "no money shall be drawn from the Treasury, but in consequence of appropriations made by law."[8] This constitutional requirement represents the corner-

---

[8] Article 1, section 9(7).

stone of control over federal spending.[9]

From January to June, Congress reviews and modifies the budget and enacts the appropriation bills for the coming year. Often, slippages occur in the congressional schedule and the full backlog of appropriations bills is not worked off until July or August and sometimes much later. In such cases temporary "continuing" appropriations are made.

The budget is not considered by the Congress as a single document nor as one piece of legislation. It is initially referred to the Appropriations Committee of the House of Representatives, where it is separated into parts, each of which is referred to a different subcommittee of the Appropriations Committee. These parts become the basis for the various appropriation bills that pass through Congress. Each subcommittee holds hearings, draws up an appropriation bill, reports it to the full Committee, and the bill proceeds through the normal legislative channels. The House of Representatives, on the basis that all "revenue" bills constitutionally must originate in the lower house, has assumed the initiating prerogative for appropriations as well as tax legislation.

The subcommittees of the Appropriations Committee, both on the House and Senate side, provide the key points of congressional control over appropriations. The Senate group generally acts as a court of appeals for the budget cuts made by the House. It has been quipped that the Senate is the Upper House because it often "ups" the appropriation bills reported by the House of Representatives.

The parent appropriations committees perform a very limited review of the recommendations of their subcommittees.[10] Ordinarily, few items actually are changed during the review of an appropriation bill on the floor of either chamber. Differences

---

[9] For an incisive treatment of the congressional review of budgetary questions, see Robert A. Wallace, *Congressional Control of Federal Spending* (Detroit: Wayne State University Press, 1960).

[10] Professor Smithies states that appropriations bills are considered by the full House Appropriations Committee "for only about an hour or so and they are usually sent unchanged to the floor of the House." Arthur Smithies, *The Budgetary Process in the United States* (New York: McGraw-Hill Book Co., 1955), p. 135.

are reconciled by a conference committee of both bodies. The President normally approves the resultant appropriation bill. Contrary to procedures of some state governments, no item vetoes of appropriation measures are authorized.

Appropriations. The total of fiscal authorizations made available to the federal agencies for a given year is composed of a number of types of enactments. The most prevalent form is the ordinary appropriation, which empowers federal agencies (1) to place orders, enter into contracts, or otherwise commit or "obligate" the government to make expenditures in the future and (2) to make the expenditures required by such obligations.

Appropriations are granted in various forms. "One-year" appropriations, which are the most common form, allow an agency to incur obligations within one fiscal year, the authority expiring at the end of the year. However, obligated balances of such appropriations remain available for two additional years for the making of expenditures. A typical example would be the funds for the General Services Administration.

"Multiple-year" appropriations are available for the incurring of obligations for a specified period of time in excess of one year, with the obligated balances likewise available for two additional years for expenditures. These appropriations may be used for programs of an unusual seasonal nature, such as the Sugar Act program of the Department of Agriculture.

"No-year" appropriations are available for both obligation and expenditure indefinitely. Military procurement and research and development are funded in this manner.

"Current indefinite" appropriations are indefinite in amount. They may be available on a one-year, multiple-year, or no-year basis. The actual amounts involved are determined in specific ways. For instance, the appropriation to the Post Office is based on the difference between postal receipts and authorized obligations.

"Permanent" appropriations are those which become available each year under existing law without new action by the Congress. They may be for definite amounts (such as the annual grant of $50,000 to each state for A&M colleges) or as indefinite as the interest required to be paid on the outstanding public debt.[11]

The last two categories of appropriations are largely immune from effective annual congressional review of the budget recommendations.

Contract Authority. Another type of financial grant is the contract authorization. This empowers the agencies only to incur obligations. In these cases, the agency has to make a later request for an appropriation to pay for or "liquidate" the obligation. Such appropriations are *pro forma* and are usually given only perfunctory review by the Congress. Appropriations to "liquidate contract authorizations" represent authority to make expenditures only, and not to incur additional obligations.

Authorizations to Expend from Debt Receipts. Authorizations to expend from debt receipts usually are used to finance lending and other government enterprises, such as the Commodity Credit Corporation. These authorizations to incur obligations and make expenditures may take the following forms:

(a) Authorization for the Treasury to make public debt receipts available for notes of the government enterprises (since the dollar balances in the bank accounts of the Treasury are not distinguishable by sources, in practice, funds obtained from taxes are lumped together with those from borrowing);

(b) Authorizations for a government enterprise to borrow directly from the public; and

(c) Cancellation of notes previously issued by a government enterprise to the Treasury (the cancellation has the effect of permitting further expenditures to be made by reason of the restoration of previously used authority to borrow from the Treasury).

The obligational authority made available is of the same character as that established by ordinary appropriations. However, authorizations to expend from debt receipts need not go through the appropriations committees nor be included in appropriation bills. Rather, they may be included in substantive legislation

---

[11] For a more technical description of the various types of new obligational authority, see *Budget of the United States Government for the Fiscal Year Ending June 30, 1964* (Washingon: U. S. Government Printing Office, 1963), pp. 126-27 (hereinafter referred to as *1964 Budget*).

reported out by committees handling the particular program and thus be immune from the annual appropriations review.

Re-authorizations. Because of the lags in the federal spending process, there are often requests to extend appropriations and other forms of obligational authority beyond the original period of enactment. The effect of such re-authorizations is the same as if new authorizations were voted in their place. Such re-authorizations generally are not included in the congressional tally of appropriations enacted and, to the extent that they are voted in lieu of new appropriations requested, often are a source of alleged "savings" by the Congress.

New Obligational Authority

The total of appropriations and other financial authorizations made available for a given year is called "new obligational authority" (see Table 6). The bulk of the grants of new obligational authority are ordinary appropriations, but, as noted above, many of them—such as permanent appropriations and authorizations to spend debt receipts—generally by-pass entirely the appropriations committees' annual review. The common characteristic of all these fiscal authorizations is that they empower the agencies to obligate the government to make expenditures in the future.

These authorizations are termed new obligational authority because they exclude the unobligated balances of prior year obligational authority which are still available for current obligation. The total of funds available for obligation, which is of importance for budgetary control, includes both new obligational authority and the unobligated balances.

The granting of new obligational authority (NOA) by the Congress is a major control point over federal spending. Given the grant of new obligational authority, the usual functioning of governmental operations will result in a subsequent flow of expenditures. Hence, to the extent that NOA is embodied in permanent authorizations, that portion of the budget is not subject to current review. To the extent that NOA is enacted by the Congress in indefinite amounts, that portion of the budget is not subject to effective review. Finally, to the extent that NOA is

31

appropriated in non-appropriation bills, that portion of the budget completely bypasses the review by the appropriations committees.

Table 6
TYPES OF NEW OBLIGATIONAL AUTHORITY
Fiscal year 1964
(billions of dollars)

Type	Current authorizations	Permanent authorizations	Total
Appropriations [1]	$96.2	$36.6	$132.8
Reappropriations	*	....	*
Authorizations to expend from dept receipts	.4	.7	1.1
Contract authorizations	*	4.9	4.9
Total [2]	$96.6	$42.2	$138.8

* Less than $50 million.
[1] Excludes appropriations to liquidate contract authorizations totaling $4.5 billion.
[2] Includes administrative budget and trust funds.
Source: *Budget of the United States Government for the Fiscal Year Ending June 30, 1964* (Washington: U. S. Government Printing Office, 1963), p. 39.

Apportionment of Funds

After the Congress has voted funds, the control over spending shifts back to the Executive Branch. The rates at which NOA is obligated are determined by the departments and agencies, subject to the control of the Bureau of the Budget, which is a staff arm of the President's office.

The Budget Bureau apportions to the agencies each quarter the funds appropriated to them. The apportionment power arises from the desire to prevent government agencies from spending their appropriations early in the year and returning for deficiency requests.[12] The apportionment process does not cover the operations of trust funds or certain government-sponsored enterprises.

The apportionment power has been used to keep the amount

---

[12] Executive Order 6166, dated June 10, 1933, gave the Bureau of the Budget the authority for making, waiving, and modifying apportionments. Previously this authority had been vested in the heads of the agencies.

of government spending for a particular item below the full limit of funds granted for it by the Congress. Although the use of apportionments for this purpose is often attacked in the legislative branch and by the potential beneficiaries of the expenditures, such use appears to be sanctioned by law.[13]

Following the making of apportionments, which is a centrally administered form of budgetary control through the Bureau of the Budget, allotments are made by department or agency heads to bureaus or other units within the agencies. Allotments may be made on a monthly or quarterly basis and may limit the use of NOA in terms of objects to be purchased, activities to be performed, or organizational units. Allotments represent an important actual or potential form of internal budgetary control within government agencies.

Incurring Obligations

Within the limits of the apportionment of funds made available to them, the federal agencies place orders, award contracts, hire personnel, and take other similar actions which commit, encumber, or "obligate" their apportioned funds. Except for a few specified instances, the law provides that "no contract for purchase is to be made except under an adequate appropriation."[14] The agencies normally obligate their available funds as rapidly as necessary to carry on their programs, limited mainly by their capability to do so.

To the extent that the goods and services needed by the government are ordered from and produced in the private economy, this is the first stage of the government spending process directly involving private industry. It is also the last step in the process in which the government has complete discretionary control over the timing of its expenditures. From this point forward, the flow of expenditures is influenced by both parties to the transactions, not merely the government.

Making Payments

Because of the multiplicity of steps involved in the federal spending process and the length of time often required by sup-

---

[13] General Appropriation Act, 1951 (64 Stat. 595).
[14] 41 U.S.C. 11; 25 U.S.C. 99.

33

pliers to produce the goods ordered by the government, there usually is a substantial lag between the time expenditures are authorized and the time they are made.

The lags in the early stages of the process are primarily administrative. It takes time for the agencies to prepare and obtain approval of their apportionment requests, for specifications to be drawn up for individual orders, and for contracts to be awarded. The lag may depend in part on the newness of the program and the necessity for establishing new procedures.

A later and more important lag is technological. It takes time for a contractor to obtain the necessary resources, to draw plans, to negotiate sub-contracts, and to solve technical difficulties. A further delay occurs after performance for delivery, inspection, paper work, and disbursements. There have been instances where payments have been delayed intentionally, particularly to defense contractors, in order to permit the government to stay within the debt ceiling during a period of seasonal pressure.

It was estimated that 52 percent of the NOA requested for the fiscal year 1964 would be spent in that year, with the remainder (except for minor amounts of lapsing appropriations) being spent in future years. Also, only 57 percent of the expenditures in that year would be made out of the authority granted in the year.[15] The remaining expenditures would come out of authority granted in prior years (see Figure 2). This indicates that the time required for effective budgetary control tends to be greater than a single fiscal year.

Reducing Governmental Spending

The actions which can be taken to curtail expenditures generally parallel the actions involved in making expenditures. A reduction in government spending can be initiated at various stages in the spending process. The effects of the actions taken at each stage can be cumulative in their effects on the total of expenditures during any given period.

By the Congress. For example, the Congress may decide to eliminate or reduce the scope of a program by (1) changing its

---

[15] *The Budget in Brief, 1964 Fiscal Year* (Washington: U. S. Government Printing Office, 1963), p. 57.

Figure 2
RELATION OF AUTHORIZATIONS TO EXPENDITURES

1964 Administrative Budget

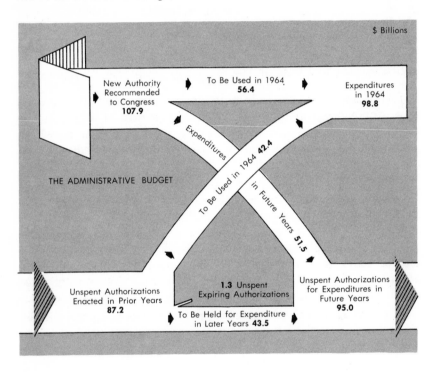

Source: U. S. Bureau of the Budget, *The Budget in Brief, Fiscal Year 1964*, (Washington: U. S. Government Printing Office, 1963), p. 57.

basic statutory authorization or (2) reducing the amount of funds authorized for it during a given period. These actions can be implemented either through eliminations or reductions in the amount of new obligational authority being considered or in the recision of existing obligational authority.

By the President. Independent of congressional action the President may decide, in view of changing circumstances and other developments, that a given agency should not utilize all of its available obligational authority. This decision can be implemented by reducing its quarterly apportionment of funds and placing a portion of the unused appropriation in "reserve."

By the Agencies. The individual agency can reduce the amount spent for a program by slowing down the rate at which it obligates its funds, by obtaining a slowdown in the rate at which particular goods or services contracted for are produced and made available to the agency, or by rescinding contracts and other commitments into which it had previously entered.

Most government contracts provide for their cancellation "in the interests of the government." However, the process of securing reductions in expenditures through cancellation of outstanding contracts has its obstacles. For example, the contractor may claim damages for the unrecoverable costs which he has incurred. Or contract cancellations may create reluctance on the part of business firms to bid on future government work.

In the case of activities such as public works projects, the desire to protect the government investment already made may be decisive in continuing expenditures on a going project in the face of a general effort to curtail goverment spending.

The Points of Control

The preceding explanation of the Federal Government spending process has pointed out the various points of control over the flow of government expenditures. Some of these control points are more effective than others. The key decision points are as follows:

1. *The enactment by the Congress of basic legislation authorizing a given government activity to be performed.* Although not

even part of the formal budgetary process, this step comes closest to being the birth stage of governmental spending. In many cases, such legislation actually contains financial authorizations, by-passing step 3, below.

2. *The review of departmental budget requests by the Bureau of the Budget and the President.* The omission of a proposed expenditure request from the President's budget means that the agency, and its clientele, will generally have an uphill fight in the Congress to add the item to the budget.

3. *The review of appropriation requests by the Congress.* The subcommittees of the House Appropriations Committee (rather than the full committee) are normally the place where the Congress gives the closest scrutiny to the individual items contained in the budget and where the bulk of changes from the President's recommendations are made. The appropriate Senate appropriations subcommittees usually provide a review of the House action. Generally, only a few items in an appropriation bill are considered individually on the floor of either House, and even fewer changes are made at that point. However, the review of appropriation requests by subcommittees and action on them by the House of Representatives and Senate as a whole represent one of the two principal points of effective budgetary control by the Congress. This is the stage at which there is a granting of the bulk of the specific new obligational authority which empowers the government agencies to set in motion a chain of action that ultimately will result in a flow of expenditures.

4. *The apportionment and allotment of funds.* The apportionment power can be and has been used to keep expenditures for a given activity below the level appropriated by the Congress. A similar result, occurring less frequently, can be obtained through the use of the allotment procedure by the head of an executive department or agency. This is the step in the process which most effectively controls the timing of the placement of contracts and the incurring of other obligations to make future expenditures.

5. *The issuance of checks by the Treasury.* Although this is the stage of the process on which public awareness of expenditures is normally focused, it is the least effective of the various points

of budgetary control. Generally, if a commitment has been made and costs incurred, the most that can be done at this stage is to postpone an expenditure. Such action often results in increasing the total cost of an operation. Where the postponement is for the purpose of slowing down the rate of expenditures, then it is an indication of ineffective budgetary control at the earlier stages of the process.

In general this review of steps in the Federal Government spending process points up the fact that if adequate controls are to be exercised over government spending, attention must be given to the early stages where programs and expenditures are authorized, rather than merely to the payments for goods and services already ordered and produced. In a more abstract way, the opportunity for free choice at any given point in time increases as we include more and more of the future within our decision-making. This may be the perennial dilemma of the "budget cutter."

THE BUILT-IN RIGIDITIES IN
THE FEDERAL BUDGET

> If a man has a limited budget to spend on cakes and
> ale, he is likely to be better satisfied if he weighs the ad-
> vantages of cakes against those of ale than if he allots
> a fixed sum to cakes and spends what is left for ale.
> —Arthur Smithies

IN THIS SECTION, a proposed federal budget is examined in
detail in terms of the leeway for effective controllability under
existing statutes and procedures. For this purpose, the budget
as originally proposed for the 1964 fiscal year is utilized, since
the proposed 1965 fiscal year budget was not available at the
time this analysis was developed.

The total amount of new obligational authority (NOA) requested in the 1964 budget came to $138.7 billion. The budget
requests of the Department of Health, Education, and Welfare

(HEW to the initiated) which sought total NOA of $23.9 billion, is selected for examination.[1] Subsequently, other departments will be examined with a view toward ascertaining the extent to which built-in rigidities exert strong influence on budget preparation and review.

Department of Health, Education, and Welfare

To provide an understanding of the problems involved, the HEW and other departmental budget requests are examined in terms of meaningful budgetary control categories, rather than by organizational units. The primary purpose is to identify the points at which the various items may be subjected to effective budgetary control—and the points at which they do not respond to review efforts.

As was pointed out earlier, NOA includes permanent and indefinite appropriations that are completely immune to annual review by the appropriations committees. Once established, these accounts do not even appear in the annual appropriations bills enacted by the Congress. Typically, the so-called "trust funds" are financed through these permanent indefinite appropriations.

It develops that HEW lays claim to the lion's share of these permanent indefinite trust funds, including the large social security trust funds as well as some smaller ones. When these automatically appropriated trust funds are deducted from the total HEW request, an interesting relationship emerges:

Line 1. Total HEW budget request $23,903,597,000
        Deduct: HEW trust funds   16,746,052,000
Line 2. Remainder of HEW budget $ 7,157,545,000

An examination of the remaining $7 billion of the almost $24 billion in the HEW budget reveals that several permanent appropriations also are included. In addition, several appropriation accounts are in the nature of charges fixed by substantive legislation. For example, the $2,950 million for grants to state governments for public assistance payments is established solely by the number of eligible persons who apply for the benefits. The substantive legislation automatically determines the share of

---

[1] The details are contained in *1964 Budget*, pp. 204-21, 311-12; Appendix, pp. 397-486.

state benefit payments which is reimbursed through these grants. Other fixed charges include the retired pay of commissioned officers of the Public Health Service and the minimum grants of $40,000 per state for library services (see Table 7 for a complete listing).

When these various fixed charges are deducted, the portion of the HEW budget subject to effective budgetary review has shrunk still further:

Line 2. (from above) $7,157,545,000
      Deduct: fixed charges   2,975,857,000
Line 3. Remainder of HEW budget $4,181,688,000

The various categories of budget requests which are not subject to effective budget scrutiny have not yet been exhausted. Public works construction projects present an especially interesting case. Typically for government agencies with lar~ ͻn-struction programs, each year's requests are domiͥ ͳ funds to continue or complete projects begun with funͫ. vided in prior year budgets. The portion of the annual buͻ̗ devoted to new construction projects is often very small. Hence, the Congress frequently is faced with the alternative of appropriating new funds for construction projects or of suffering the loss of the investment already made. (For example, what is the use of half a bridge?) HEW does not rank high in the roster of federal agencies in terms of its construction programs. However, if account is taken of the portion of the HEW request earmarked for continuation of construction work previously started, the controllable portion of the budget is reduced further:

Line 3. (from above) $4,181,688,000
      Deduct: continuing construction   18,007,000
Line 4. Remainder of HEW budget $4,163,681,000

Finally, there is a category of budget requests which, although subject to review by the appropriations committees, are not included in the annual appropriations bills. These are the supplementals which often contain the budgetary requests formally submitted, relatively late in the congressional session, after new substantive laws are enacted by the Congress. Although these supplemental requests are considered by the appropriations committees and subcommittees of the Congress, they are not included in the detailed review of an agency's program and activities which the Congress performs in connection with the annual appropriations bills. When these supplementals are deducted, a fairly good estimate of that portion of the HEW budget which is subject to effective budgetary control is obtained:

Line 4. (from above) $4,163,681,000
         Deduct: supplementals   1,619,000,000

Line 5. HEW budget request subject
         to effective review $2,544,681,000

Table 7

DEPARTMENT OF HEALTH, EDUCATION, AND WELFARE

1964 Budget Request

(thousands of dollars)

Trust Funds
Federal old-age and survivors insurance $15,568,910
Disability insurance trust fund 1,176,838
Miscellaneous 304

Subtotal, trust funds $16,746,052

Fixed Charges
Minimum endowments for A&M colleges .... $ 7,650
Minimum grants for library services 2,060
Endowment for A&M colleges (permanent) 2,550
Vocational education grants (permanent) 7,161
Retired pay of commissioned officers (indefinite)................ 6,436
Grants for public assistance 2,950,000

Subtotal, fixed charges .... $ 2,975,857

Continuing Construction Work
Public Health Service work previously started................... $ 13,487
Howard University work previously started 4,520

Subtotal, continuing construction work .... $ 18,007

Proposed Legislation
To be contained in supplemental appropriation bills .... $ 1,619,000

Balance
Budget request subject to effective review .... $ 2,544,681

Total new obligational authority $23,903,597

Dimensions of the cumulative impact of the various items relatively immune to budgetary review thus become apparent (see Table 7). According to these calculations, out of a total HEW budget for the fiscal year 1964 of $23.9 billion, only $2.5 billion, or 11 percent, was subject to effective annual budgetary control by the Congress.

It is true that the Congress may, and often does, reduce through the appropriation process, appropriations requests of the type classified here as non-controllable. For example, the Congress might reduce the requested appropriation for public assistance grants to states, reasoning that the requested figure is larger than required to meet obligations. However, the reductions of the appropriation will not in itself reduce the obligations. If the reduced appropriation later proves to be inadequate, the necessity for a supplemental appropriation will arise and its enactment will be routine.

In order to illustrate other patterns that exist, another agency, the Department of the Interior, is analyzed next. While the bulk of HEW expenditures is devoted to grants to states and social security benefit payments, Interior is primarily concerned with large construction projects and other efforts to develop or conserve the nation's natural resources.

Department of the Interior

Interior's requested NOA for 1964 came to $1,348 million,[2] about one-twentieth of HEW's budget. However, unlike HEW, only a small proportion of this budget request was for trust funds. The $70 million of such trust fund appropriations mainly cover required payments to Indian tribal funds.

Line 1.	Total Interior budget request	$1,348,163,000
	Deduct: trust funds	69,570,000
Line 2.	Remainder of Interior budget	$1,278,593,000

Like HEW, a number of Interior appropriations are of the permanent variety, such as those for claims and treaty obligations. Although these fixed charges are not of the same absolute size as the ones examined previously, they form a significant proportion of the Interior budget request:

---

[2] The details are contained in *1964 Budget*, pp. 221-44, 313; Appendix, pp. 487-576.

Line 2. (from above) $1,278,593,000
         Deduct: fixed charges   263,743,000

Line 3. Remainder of Interior budget $1,014,850,000

Unlike the welfare agency, the Department of the Interior carries on many relatively large construction programs, such as those of the Bureau of Reclamation. The 1964 budget contains requests to continue numerous construction projects of the Reclamation Bureau and the Southwestern Power Administration previously started. When these continuing commitments are taken into account, the Interior budget subject to effective control diminishes sharply:

Line 3. (from above) $1,014,850,000
         Deduct: continuing construction
         work   321,062,000

Line 4. Remainder of Interior budget $693,788,000

Finally, the Interior budget included a relatively small amount for proposed legislation which would be financed through a supplemental appropriation bill, rather than the regular appropriations subject to close congressional scrutiny:

Line 4. (from above) $693,788,000
         Deduct: proposed legislation   25,000,000

Line 5. Interior budget request subject
         to effective review $668,788,000

To recapitulate, out of a total recommended budget for the Department of the Interior of $1.3 billion, only $669 million or 49 percent is subject to effective annual budgetary control by the Congress (see Table 8).

Other Agencies

The Departments of the Interior and Health, Education, and Welfare are by no means atypical in conducting many programs largely immune to budgetary review. The great bulk of the Treasury Department's expenditures, for example, are made under permanent indefinite appropriations to pay the interest due on the national debt.[3] The greater part of the Veterans Administration's budget is devoted to payments of pensions and compensation to eligible veterans. The eligibility is determined by the basic statutes on veterans' benefits and the actual expenditures for a given year depend on the number of qualified veterans who apply for these payments. In years when the Congress initially appropriates too low an amount for this program, subsequent supplemental appropriations are routinely enacted.

Also, 91 percent of the Labor Department's budget is for the permanent indefinite appropriations for the unemployment trust funds. Table 9 shows, for the various major agencies, the limited extent to which their funds are subject to effective congressional budgetary review. The concepts used in preparing these estimates are the same as those used for the Interior and HEW budgets analyzed above. In all borderline and doubtful cases, the programs were classified as controllable.

Table 8
DEPARTMENT OF THE INTERIOR
1964 Budget Request
(thousands of dollars)

Trust Funds	
Indian tribal funds	$ 60,389
Miscellaneous	9,181
Subtotal, trust funds	$ 69,570
Fixed Charges	
Indefinite appropriations of fees and charges	$ 117,766
Public land roads and trails (permanent)	4,000
Claims and treaty obligations (permanent)	161
Other permanent, indefinite, special accounts	137,191
Required lead and zinc subsidies	4,625
Subtotal, fixed charges	$ 263,743
Continuing Construction Work	
Reclamation projects previously started	$ 218,053
Upper Colorado River storage project	99,100
Southwestern power construction	3,909
Subtotal, continuing construction work	$ 321,062
Proposed Legislation	
To be contained in supplemental appropriation bills	$ 25,000
Balance	
Budget request subject to effective review	$ 668,788
Total new obligational authority	$ 1,348,163

---

[3] For a complete listing of permanent and indefinite appropriations, see U. S. Congress, *Appropriations, Budget Estimates, etc.,* Senate Document No. 162, 87th Congress, 2d Session (Washington: U. S. Government Printing Office, 1962), pp. 678-97, 708-15.

Table 9

SUMMARY ANALYSIS OF 1964 BUDGET REQUESTS

(millions of dollars)

Agency	Requested NOA	Not subject to effective review	Subject to effective review Amount	Percent
Domestic-civilian				
Dept. of Agriculture..	$ 8,195	$ 4,288	$ 3,907	48
Dept of Commerce	4,696	3,715	981	21
Dept. of Health, Education, and Welfare	23,904	21,360.	2,544	11
Dept. of the Interior..	1,348	679	669	49
Dept. of Labor	4,815	4,388	427	9
Treasury Dept.	11,318	10,124	1,194	11
Veterans Administration	6,310	4,755	1,555	25
All Other Agencies....	10,475	5,461	5,014	48
Subtotal	$ 71,061	$54,770	$16,291	23
Security-related				
Dept. of Defense	$ 52,181	$ 2,063	$50,118	96
Dept. of Justice	355	....	355	100
Dept. of State	374	2	372	99
Funds appropriated to the President......	6,154	956	5,198	84
Atomic Energy Commission	2,893	....	2,893	100
National Aeronautics and Space Administration	5,712	....	5,712	100
Subtotal	$ 67,669	$ 3,021	$64,648	96
Grand total	$138,730	$57,791	$80,939	58

Source: *Budget of the United States Government for the Fiscal Year Ending June 30, 1964* (Washington: U. S. Government Printing Office, 1963) and Appendix.

Overall, it is estimated that only 58 percent of requested new spending authority in the 1964 budget was subject to effective review. However, as may be seen in Table 10, there are two different categories of federal agencies involved. Those agencies and departments most closely related to the national security, such as the Department of Defense, NASA, and the AEC, have very few permanent appropriations, trust funds, or other fixed charges. On the average, 96 percent of the expenditure authorizations of these agencies is subject to effective annual control. In striking contrast, only 23 percent of the new spending authority in the other agency budgets—devoted principally to domestic civilian programs—is actually subject to effective review (see Figure 3). The bulk of the expenditures for these civilian-program agencies is authorized virtually automatically as a result of the basic, continuing commitments contained in statutes generally written by and reported out to the floor of the House and Senate by committees of the Congress concerned with the individual program rather than with the state of federal finances.[4]

The foregoing analysis may help to explain the sense of futility on the part of many persons and organizations who have attempted to develop recommendations for comprehensive revisions in the presidential budget recommendations of a given year. The birth stage of much of Federal Government spending, as previously pointed out, is not at the point where appropriations are voted but at the earlier point where the Congress enacts the basic legislative commitment. The most effective point of control is at this earlier stage in the government spending process.[5] Indeed, much of the folklore concerning the uncontrollability of government spending could be eliminated if actions were to be taken on the basis of a proper understanding of the cycle of government spending—which is a far greater period than a single fiscal year. Subsequent sections of this study explore methods of attacking this problem.

Need for Congressional Review of Fixed Budget Items

At this point it is appropriate to ask: "What may be done about the already built-in rigidities of the federal budget?"

Obviously, there are certain naturally uncontrollable items about which little, if anything, may be done. The prime example

---

[4] For an earlier attempt at analyzing the controllability of federal spending, but limited to the administrative budget, see "Controllability of 1952 Budget Expenditures," in Joint Committee on the Economic Report, U. S. Congress, *January 1951 Economic Report of the President* (Washington: U. S. Government Printing Office, 1951), pp. 89-103.

[5] Compare Professor Smithies' statement, "The point to emphasize is that the rates of expenditure are virtually settled by the Veterans' Affairs Committee of the Congress, and its function is to put forward the needs of the veterans rather than to consider the relations of the veterans' program to other programs and to the budget as a whole. The latter function is not performed at all in the Congress." Smithies, *op. cit.*, p. 381.

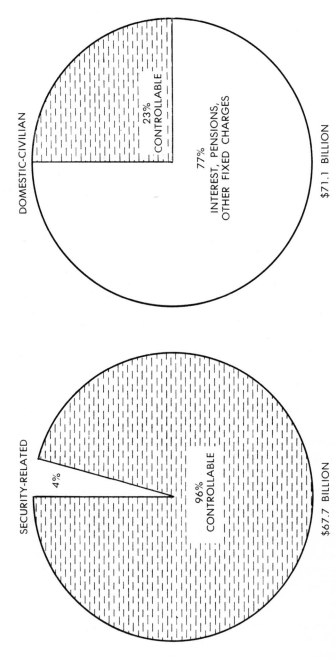

Figure 3

Controllability of 1964 Federal Budget

DOMESTIC-CIVILIAN

23% CONTROLLABLE

77% INTEREST, PENSIONS, OTHER FIXED CHARGES

$71.1 BILLION

SECURITY-RELATED

4%

96% CONTROLLABLE

$67.7 BILLION

NEW OBLIGATIONAL AUTHORITY: ADMINISTRATIVE + TRUST FUNDS

here is the interest on the public debt which, to express the situation in simple terms, just has to be paid. In this instance, the possibility for reduction lies not in appropriating action or in changes in substantive legislation, but in reduction in the amount of the debt upon which interest is payable.

However, with respect to the bulk of the remaining fixed-cost budget items, there are at least two re-examination approaches which the Executive Branch and/or the Congress, if they were so-minded, might undertake:

1. A survey of all basic laws establishing the fixed obligations in order to identify programs and expenditure items that, through substantive law changes, properly might be converted to an annual budgetary review status.

2. Further examination of fixed-expenditure programs still not susceptible to annual review to determine whether, in the light of the total federal budget problem, certain changes in basic formulas, eligibility rules, or other conditions controlling amounts of expenditures might be desirable.

The objective of a survey of the type described first above would be to seek out permanent expenditure programs wherein conditions have changed to such an extent as to make annual budgetary review the more logical course. A possible example is the program established by section 32 of the Act of August 24, 1935,[6] under which an amount equal to 30 percent of annual customs receipts is automatically appropriated into a permanent, indefinite fund for the "removal of surplus agricultural commodities." These amounts obviously bear little relationship to the "need" for such funds, and recent appropriation acts have authorized transfers of section 32 funds to the school lunch program for the purchase and distribution of agricultural commodities, a program which is itself under annual budgetary review.

Annual grants of $50,000 paid to each state and Puerto Rico for A&M colleges similarly are made under a permanent appropriation act. The Congress has no opportunity to review the annual appropriation request and thus to determine the continued

---

[6] U.S.C. 612c. The portion of these funds allocable to fishery products is transferred to the Department of the Interior to encourage the distribution of U. S. fishery products.

need for or desirability of these payments. There are other examples, such as permanent indefinite appropriations for the Department of the Interior which are tied to a portion of revenues from sales or rentals of government assets and bear little if any relationship to the current requirements for federal expenditures. In this connection, visitor fees at Yellowstone National Park are used automatically to finance educational expenses of dependents of park personnel, while visitor fees at Grand Teton National Park are used for payments to the State of Wyoming, in effect, in lieu of taxes.

Conceivably, many of the statutory requirements of the nature described may have outlived their original purpose of usefulness, and, at a minimum, might be replaced by permissive, authorizing legislation which would require annual congressional action on appropriation requests.

If the second suggested survey were to be carried out, it obviously would constitute a congressional study of major proportions. If set up on a full-scale basis, it would deal with basic laws controlling the operation of programs such as the highway aid program, social security benefits, veterans' compensation payments, unemployment compensation, numerous kinds of grants-in-aid, and various subsidy programs.

The purpose could be to subject to a coordinated review all of the programs for which the granting of appropriations, because of controlling conditions in basic law, is now a perfunctory and automatic process. In this instance, the controlling conditions would in themselves be the objects of the study.

Such a study would deal with many government programs which, from a political standpoint, are considered to be highly sensitive. Involved would be complications stemming from long-standing jurisdictional perogatives of congressional committees. The undertaking admittedly would be a difficult one.

Nevertheless, the Congress appears to be confronted with the alternatives either of performing periodically such a re-examination of its fixed-cost commitments, or of permitting an already-established 40 percent or more of the fiscal program of the Federal Government to ride along in permanent immunity from effective congressional control.

PROPOSED LEGISLATION: BIRTH STAGE OF GOVERNMENT SPENDING

AS NOTED PREVIOUSLY, the enactment of basic or substantive legislation is the birth stage of new government expenditure programs. Customarily, a variety of such proposals is recommended to the Congress each year. For example, the 1964 fiscal year budget revealed at least 35 identifiable proposals under different budget headings which would commit or authorize expenditures in future years.[1] Additional expenditure proposals, not included in budget submission, always may be effectively initiated from other sources during a congressional session.

---

[1] These items are shown in *1964 Budget*, pp. 7-34, 60-111.

Some of the 35 legislative proposals identified in the 1964 budget have been approved in original or altered form, and others either rejected or allowed to remain pending, during the course of the calendar year 1963 congressional session. However, since the disposition made of individual proposals is not pertinent for purposes of this study, the 35 are hereafter listed and discussed without regard to actions taken on them during 1963.

About one-third of the 35 proposals would have established entirely new government programs, such as the following (1964 NOA request shown in parenthesis where identifiable):

1. A national Academy of Foreign Affairs.
2. Grants to colleges and universities for work in the area of natural resources.
3. Grants to states for water resources planning.
4. Grants to states for planning outdoor recreation and for acquiring recreational lands ($25 million).
5. Federal aid for urban mass transportation ($100 million).
6. Grants for construction of new medical, dental, osteopathic and public health schools and aid to medical and dental students ($34 million).
7. A "long-range" effort to stimulate development of mental health facilities and services.
8. A youth employment program ($100 million).
9. A National Service Corps ("domestic peace corps").
10. A new general education program ($1,215 million).
11. New bureaus of community health and environment health.
12. Health insurance for the aged.

Many of these legislative authorizations would have been permissive rather than mandatory. Nevertheless, if enacted, they could be considered to be moral commitments upon the Congress to fund the respective activities at "good-faith" performance levels. Whatever expenditure levels that might be voted would then be incorporated in the new base line of federal spending.

Many of the 35 legislative proposals reflected in the 1964 budget would have extended expiring programs or increased the authorized size and scope of existing programs. Examples include the following:

1. To increase the rates of military pay ($900 million).
2. To provide additional office and housing facilities for the State Department.
3. To extend the foreign aid program for another year.
4. To eliminate the annual ceiling of $10 million on the budget of the Arms Control and Disarmament Agency ($5 million).
5. To continue the food stamp program ($25 million).
6. To provide further federal acquisitions of land "to protect wilderness areas of great natural beauty."
7. To increase the maximum limits on federal loans and grants under the area redevelopment program.
8. To extend the federal grant-in-aid program for airport construction beyond 1964.
9. To increase the maximum authorization for loans to provide housing for elderly and moderate-income persons.
10. To broaden financial aid to hospitals ($35 million).
11. To increase federal participation in prevention and control of air pollution.
12. To extend assistance to schools in federally affected areas ($254 million).
13. To increase the government contribution and make other changes in the Civil Service Retirement and Disability Fund.
14. To enable the Secretary of Agriculture to stockpile food for civil defense ($30 million).
15. General farm legislation.
16. To shift the farm housing loan program from direct to insured loans ($105 million).
17. To extend the life of the Export-Import Bank for five years.
18. To increase benefits for children and dependent parents of veterans who died as a result of military service.
19. To make permanent "improvements" in the unemployment insurance program.
20. To get the railroad retirement and unemployment insurance systems out of "financial difficulties."
21. To promote maternal and child health ($17 million).

22. To extend the life of the Civil Rights Commission beyond November 30, 1963.

Finally, one of the 35 proposals simply would have exempted an existing program from annual budgetary review. This concerned the Rural Electrification Administration of the Department of Agriculture, which under current rules had been depositing the repayments it received on loans directly into the Federal Treasury. Consequently, new loans have been dependent upon appropriations voted by the Congress. The proposed legislation would have permitted the REA to keep the repayments it received on old loans and use the proceeds to make new loans without further congressional review and approval.

To indicate the fiscal consequences of a "want" list of proposed legislation creating expenditure obligations there is available an old but still useful study prepared by the Bureau of the Budget. This study identifies the portion of expenditure estimates in the 1952 budget, presented to the first session of the 82d Congress, which resulted from legislation enacted by the 80th and 81st Congresses alone. The total came to $7.6 billion of expenditures in an estimated total of $71.6 billion, or more than 10 percent. Eighteen pages of fine print were required to list the various items of new legislation which had been added to the budget during the period covered.[2]

Both the new and old lists of increments to legislative authorizations for government spending programs have a common characteristic in that they would reduce the controllable portion of future budgets. For example, in the case of the first item on the 1964 list—the establishment of a National Academy of Foreign Affairs—the enactment of basic authorizing legislation would at least morally commit future sessions of the Congress to provide funds for such an academy at some minimum level. Another item, the proposed military pay rate increases, would be a relatively fixed charge on the budget, annual congressional discretion being limited to the total payroll cost to be allowed.

Yet from another viewpoint, proposed legislation represents that stage of the overall Federal Government spending process which is most amendable to direct and effective control. At the

---

[2] *January 1951 Economic Report of the President, op. cit.,* pp. 48-67.

outset, the President can refrain from making these new recommendations, or he may modify proposals of administrative agencies to his liking. The Congress can refuse to vote enabling legislation, or modify proposals as its collective judgment dictates. Finally, the President can veto any such legislation that is passed by the Congress.

THE CHOICE AMONG
ALTERNATIVES

Congress never has an opportunity to consider the budget as a whole and weigh the relative needs of all programs. Thus the central purpose of the budget process is largely defeated. —Joseph P. Harris

A GREAT DEAL has been written in the literature on public administration and public finance to the effect that the essence of budgeting is the choice among alternatives.[1] This section is devoted to an empirical attempt at reclassifying budget recommen-

[1] "Budgeting is essentially an economic problem, in solving as it does the allocation of scarce resources among almost insatiable and competing demands," Smithies, *op. cit.*, pp. XIV-XV; ". . . the primary purpose of budgeting ought to be to achieve the most desirable allocation of funds among alternative uses," Edward C. Banfield, "Congress and The Budget: A Planner's Criticism," *American Political Science Review*, December 1949, pp. 1217-18.

dations in a manner to illustrate how practical application may be made of the choice-among-alternatives principle.

Rather than to utilize the existing agency or functional classifications, let us return to first principles. What are the major end purposes for which the various government programs are carried on?

In a world of critical international tensions, the initial purpose that comes to mind is the protection of the nation against external aggressors—to maintain the national security. A variety of programs is suggested, ranging from the equipping and maintaining of our own military establishment and the bolstering of the armed forces of other nations regarded as potential allies, to various types of nonmilitary competition.

A second basic national purpose, one also going back to the Constitution, is the promotion of the public welfare. Here, under the public welfare interpretation that has prevailed, we find the Federal Government operating in the fields of health, pensions, unemployment compensation, relief, and many other such activities.

A third major purpose of government programs has received an increasing amount of attention in recent years—economic development. This area covers the various programs to develop natural resources and transportation, as well as to support education and to attempt to quicken the growth rate of the national economy.

Finally, we have the routine day-to-day operation of the government, such as the functioning of the Congress and the federal courts, the collection of revenues, and the payment of interest on the national debt.

Table 10 shows how the requested funds in the 1964 budget, utilized here for illustrative purposes, were allocated among the four major purposes outlined above. It may come as no surprise that a large portion of the budget—but less than one-half—is devoted to the national security. In contrast, the fact that the great bulk of all non-military spending is devoted to the various welfare programs may not be as widely known. A comparatively small portion is devoted to economic development and, as may be observed, even some of the latter programs may be quite questionable as to their positive effect on the growth and development of the nation.

An examination of the various budgetary documents over the years reveals little systematic attempt to appraise the wisdom or desirability of the overall choice implicitly made in the allocation of government resources among the major alternative uses. It may be mere conjecture to conclude that, possibly, the allocation would have been somewhat different if the appropriation reviews had been approached from this viewpoint. However, added insight to the possible program choices that can be made may be gained from a somewhat deeper analysis of the content of each of these categories.

Table 10

PROGRAM COMPOSITION OF THE 1964 BUDGET
(New Obligational Authority)

Broad Purpose	Amount (millions)	Percent
National security	$ 63,904	46
Public welfare	46,885	34
Economic development	14,296	10
Government operations	13,645	10
Total	$138,730	100

Source: Appendix B, p. 89.

National Security

As would be expected, the bulk of the national security budget was devoted to the U. S. military forces. However, about one-fifth of the total was comprised of programs that would have promoted the national security through somewhat more indirect means, such as non-military forms of competition (NASA and USIA), or bolstering of military capabilities of friendly nations.

The data in Table 11 may be used to indicate the types of "strategic" choices which can be made—or are currently made by default, or accident—in the allocation of funds for national security. First of all, these various programs, in a practical sense, are not now brought together and viewed as a totality anywhere in the congressional review phase of the budgeting process. Hopefully, the approach suggested here would lend itself to first raising and then answering questions such as the following:

Would the national security be improved by shifting some or all of the $12 billion for foreign aid and non-military competition to the U. S. military establishment itself?

Table 11
NATIONAL SECURITY PROGRAMS
1964 Budget

Program category	Amount (millions)	Percent
U. S. military forces	$51,473	80.6
Scientific competition (NASA)	5,712	9.0
Foreign non-military aid	4,689	7.3
Foreign military forces	1,480	2.3
U. S. passive defense	318	.5
Political and psychological competition (USIA)	217	.3
Arms control and disarmament	15	*
Total	$63,904	100.0

* Less than .05 percent.

Conversely, would the national security be strengthened by moving a proportionately small share of the direct military budget, say $500 million, to USIA or the arms control effort, thus to produce proportionately large increases in these latter programs?

Are we putting too much into foreign economic aid and not enough into the Voice of America (USIA)? Or vice versa?

Would we be better off if we shifted the funds now going to passive (civil) defense to the U. S. Arms Control and Disarmament Agency? Or vice versa?

Utilization of the type of approach suggested here may lead not only to attempts to answer questions such as these but, more fundamentally, to widen the horizons of budget reviewers.

Public Welfare

As shown in Table 10, about one-third of requested new obligational authority in the 1964 budget was devoted to programs in the general area of the public welfare. Although the reader may wish to challenge, or change, the classification of some of these items, the tabulation of public welfare programs in Table 12 illustrates the assortment of choices that are made as to uses to which public funds are to be put.

The several social insurance and retirement programs receive the bulk of the funds for public welfare. However, this is hardly a conscious decision. As pointed out earlier, the expenditures for these programs—such as the old-age and survivors insurance systems—are determined by basic statute and generally are not even reviewable during the appropriations process. For this and other reasons, it should not be surprising that they have grown to dominate the nondefense budget, with their commitments exceeding by a wide margin the total for the various economic development programs (see Table 13, below).

Likewise, the commitments under the various agricultural price support programs (in the category of "assistance to farmers and rural areas") exceed all of the programs of urban housing and facilities. Again, the farm subsidy program is generally set by substantive law, rather than through annual appropriations.

This level of detail also permits some cross-comparisons of government programs between the "national security" and "public welfare" categories. For example, the $7.2 billion for aid to farmers is roughly equal to the total allocated for civilian space exploration ($5.7 billion) plus foreign military assistance ($1.5 billion). Would some trade-off between the public welfare and national security areas result in a net advantage? Again, we are trying to answer the question, "Would an extra dollar (a billion, in the case of the government) be more wisely spent for program A or for program B?" This is the fundamental question implicit in the allocation of budgetary funds or any other resources. The literally thousands of pages of budget justifications and congressional hearings which are published each year fail to show even any awareness of the problem, much less any attempt at an answer.

Yet, it is suggested that the approach described here would be useful in attempting to achieve various basic aims through the budgetary process. For one thing, an attempt to balance the outgo side against projected revenues might be more successfully accomplished than in the past through this process of weighing alternative programs against each other and choosing the more useful or higher priority items. Similarly, during an inflationary period, increases in federal revenues might be consciously allocated between say, greater welfare and faster economic growth—or even might be utilized for debt retirement—

rather than to be used up through an unplanned addition of unrelated individual appropriations.

Table 12
PUBLIC WELFARE PROGRAMS
1964 Budget

Program category	Amount (millions)	Percent
Social insurance and retirement	$22,314	47.6
Aid to farmers and rural areas	7,290	15.5
Public assistance	4,919	10.5
Unemployment insurance	4,407	9.4
Health	3,084	6.6
Veterans compensation	2,061	4.4
Urban housing and facilities	1,667	3.6
Other welfare	1,143	2.4
Total	$46,885	100.0

Economic Development

In the exploratory categorization of government programs presented here, various activities are listed under the heading "Economic Development" (see Table 13). Judgments may differ, of course, as to whether certain of the programs involved here actually contribute to the more rapid growth and development of the American economy. The very existence of sharp judgment differences, however, emphasizes the need for better means of evaluating the worth of the respective programs.

A brief examination of the composition of the economic development category may be revealing. Transportation facilities account for the largest single share and, when combined with natural resource programs, account for fully two-thirds of the total.

Table 13
ECONOMIC DEVELOPMENT PROGRAMS
1964 Budget

Program category	Amount (millions)	Percent
Transportation facilities	$ 5,066	35.5
Natural resources	4,484	31.4
Education and general research	2,839	19.8
Aids and subsidies to business	1,743	12.2
Economic regulation	164	1.1
Total	$14,296	100.0

A further breakdown also indicates another level of trade-offs which is possible. The amount shown for transportation facilities consists of three types of programs, as follows (in millions) :

Land transportation	$3,892
Air transportation	810
Water transportation	364
Total	$5,066

The dominance of land transportation, mainly the federal-aid highway program, is striking. It accounts for over 76 percent of the transportation total. Would a revised trade-off between land and air transport expenditures be advisable? Between land transportation ($3.9 billion) and education and general research ($2.8 billion) ? Raising these questions should not be taken as expressing value judgments, but rather as indicating a pattern for decision-making.

As indicated previously, some programs included under the economic development category may be questionable as to their economic benefits. In the case of natural resource programs, the bulk of the funds is devoted to the dams, power, and related multi-purpose projects of the Corps of Engineers and the Bureau of Reclamation. Yet many authorities question the merits of individual projects.

Professor Otto Eckstein of Harvard University concluded in a study published by the congressional Joint Economic Committee in 1957:

> In the case of at least half of all the projects that are being built, it is unlikely that their effect on national income will be positive. . . . The return on many projects is so low that their net effect will be to reduce the rate of growth of the economy.[2]

Professor Eckstein pointed out that the techniques used by federal agencies to measure benefits from water resource projects "considerably overstate the additions to national income" by inflating the indirect or secondary benefits which might accrue from the expenditure.[3] However, a more basic shortcoming of

---

[2] Otto Eckstein, "Evaluation of Federal Expenditures for Water Resource Projects," in Joint Economic Committee, U. S. Congress, *Federal Expenditure Policy for Economic Growth and Stability* (Washington: U. S. Government Printing Office, 1957), p. 667.

[3] *Ibid.*, pp. 658-59.

these projects may be the contribution they make to the large farm surpluses—accomplished through the expanding of the land areas on which farm products, not needed to meet consumer demands at current prices, are being grown.

Here there appears the possibility of an unusual agricultural-resource trade-off in which, to some extent, a reduction in funds for natural resources would permit a reduction in farm subsidy outlays. This illustrates another aspect of the broadening of the vista of budgetary review. Not only can we examine choices among programs, but we can also examine the consistency of the various programs in relation to each other.

Government Operations

The final category of government programs represents, as best may be estimated, the general costs of operating the government in its routine, day-to-day functions. Table 14 shows that approximately three-fourths of the funds in this category covered the permanent indefinite appropriation for the payment of interest on the public debt. The bulk of the remaining one-fourth of the outlays for government operations was devoted to collection of internal revenue and the housekeeping functions of the General Services Administration, such as the Public Buildings Service and the Federal Supply Service.

Table 14
GOVERNMENT OPERATIONS
1964 Budget

Program category	Amount (millions)	Percent
Interest payments	$10,103	74.1
Housekeeping functions	2,578	18.8
Judicial and law enforcement	430	3.2
Conducting foreign relations	411	3.0
Legislative functions	123	.9
Total	$13,645	100.0

Utilization of the Purpose Approach

To some extent, the material in this section properly may be criticized as being essentially "just another functional classification of budget programs." This would miss the point. The present functional classification used in the federal budget (see Table 2) is merely a reporting device and not a mechanism for decision-making in the actual budgetary process. The Congress is well aware of this situation and, except as to the rough paralleling of government functions and appropriation subcommittee assignments in a very gross manner, largely avoids the functional classifications.

The theme of this section, in contrast, is that the budgetary process itself should make use of a program or purpose approach to decision-making. To some extent, in response to recommendations of various Hoover Commission reports [4] and others, a purpose approach to federal budgeting has been utilized in recent years. However, it has been used solely to review detailed activities comprising a single appropriation account (e.g., civil actions versus criminal actions in the Department of Justice's legal staff). It is suggested here that the purpose approach be broadened to cover basic functions and purposes for which the detailed government activities have been instituted in the first place (see Appendix B, p. 89 for program composition of the 1964 budget).

This may be an instance where the public may respond to a proper presentation of the alternatives. A recent detailed study of public attitudes toward government spending programs indicated that a clear majority of the sample of persons interviewed believed increases in one area of government spending should be offset by commensurate decreases in other areas, rather than being additive.

The following specific question was posed: "If the cold war with Russia should cost us more money during the next few years, do you think the government should raise taxes or spend less on other things, or go further into debt?"

Approximately 62 percent of the sample preferred spending less on other government programs, rather than either increases in taxes (29 percent) or deficit financing (4 percent). Also, some were uncertain or otherwise qualified their views.[5]

---

[4] U. S. Commission of Organization of the Executive Branch of the Government, *Budgeting and Accounting* (Washington: U. S. Government Printing Office, 1949), pp. 7-17, 77-84.

[5] Eva Mueller, "Public Attitudes Toward Fiscal Programs," *Quarterly Journal of Economics*, May 1963, p. 218.

During the last few years, there has been one very good example of congressional interest and concern with a functional or purpose approach to budgeting. In the case of the Department of Defense, the Executive Branch has made the basic budget decisions via such an end-purpose approach.

Although military appropriation requests still are submitted on the basis of operations and maintenance, personnel, procurement, and similar classifications, the underlying decisions are made on a program basis. Here it is a question, for example, of strategic versus limited war capability—or offensive versus defensive forces. Within such overall categories, the alternative weapon systems which could fulfill the same end mission are compared with each other.[6] One case would be the Navy's Polaris missile system competing with the Air Force's Minuteman ICBM for strategic funds without regard to the necessary crossing of the organizational lines of the two services. (In earlier years it was more a case of the Navy's strategic missiles competing with Marine Corps ordnance—two relatively unrelated items—within the Naval procurement budget.)

The advantage of this new method of budget presentation is that it permits direct comparison of the various programs of the different services which are close substitutes for each other or which contribute to a common mission or purpose. Clearly, this is a general methodology which has application in budgeting for nonmilitary programs.

Recent military appropriations and authorization hearings and reports show increased congressional attention to the new program approach to military budgeting. This may not be surprising in view of the fact that the Secretary of Defense uses this approach in presenting his major recommendations and supporting analyses.

It may be reasonable to assume that the incorporation in the Budget Message and the Budget Document of the approach here suggested might result in growing congressional and public interest. Alternatively, a congressional committee staff could re-

---

[6] Cf. David Novick, "Planning Ahead in the Department of Defense," *California Management Review*, Summer 1963, pp. 35-42. Mr. Novick's initial treatment of this subject is contained in Rand Corporation Report 254, *Efficiency and Economy in Government Through New Budgeting and Accounting Procedures*, February 1, 1954.

work the existing budget submissions within this framework for review, say, by the entire appropriations committees prior to their detailed review of individual appropriation requests. This might permit the parent appropriations committees to set general guidelines and ground rules for detailed budgetary review. This would be quite different from the present situation where the overall allocation of budgetary funds among the major functions of government is more nearly the accidental result of a myriad of individual budget decisions.

Hopefully, this suggested procedure might permit the Congress to exercise the role in budgetary review envisioned by Professor Harris:

> . . . instead of attempting to decide whether an activity could be carried on as well with fewer employees or less expenditures for supplies, automobiles, postage, or public relations, it should give more attention to whether the program is needed at all, or whether the money could be better spent for something else.[7]

The Choice of Not to Spend

Up to this point, the exploratory treatment of the subject of budgetary alternatives has been limited chiefly to examinations of trade-offs in expenditures among programs, based upon evaluations of the worth of end purposes to be served. This emphasis on choices among programs has been for the purpose of explanation and illustration of the principle involved, but the treatment given to the subject is not intended to imply that another kind of choice is not available.

The basic choice in any budgetary decision, obviously, is whether funds that would be required for a given purpose should be spent at all. Would the national welfare be benefited more by an increase in private spending (perhaps fostered by a reduction in tax rates) than by an increment in governmental expenditures?

---

[7] Harris, *op. cit.*

THE SEARCH FOR IMPROVEMENTS
IN BUDGET-CONTROL TECHNIQUES

> At a certain village in La Mancha, which I shall not
> name, there liv'd not long ago one of those old-fashion'd
> gentlemen who are never without a Lance Upon a Rock,
> an old Target, a lean Horse, and a Greyhound.
> —Miguel de Cervantes

IN THE COURSE of consideration of both the expenditure and revenue aspects of the 1964 fiscal year budget, and in preparatory steps looking toward a new budget year, there has been a marked intensification of attention to the question of federal expenditure control.

Should the Congress determine to undertake a serious, intensified search for improvements in budget-control techniques, it will be able to take advantage of much exploration in the past toward this objective.

Over the years, numerous proposals have been made for improvement of congressional review of the federal budget. Suggestions along these lines have been made by both advocates of greater economy and proponents of new or expanded government spending programs.

It is true that despite the variety of the proposals there has been, since the enactment of the historic Budget and Accounting Act of 1921, only slight modifications of the way in which the Congress acts on the budget.

The fact remains, as shown in this study, that serious weaknesses exist in the means at the command of the Congress to exercise effective budgetary control on a coordinated basis and in accordance with the basic purposes of budgeting. The need is for improvements that will better equip the Congress (1) to make budget-oriented judgments at the authorization, or birth-stage level of expenditure programs, (2) to arrive at an evaluation of individual expenditures from a total-budget viewpoint, and (3) to utilize knowledgeably the opportunity through the budgeting process to choose among the various purposes for which given amounts of funds can be spent.

Organization for Budgetary Control

Of the many suggestions for budgeting improvements that have been made over the years, the great majority consists of proposals to change the congressional organization for budgetary control. Emerson Schmidt has stated that "one of the major difficulties to sound Congressional control over budget matters stems from the manner in which its committee structure is organized." [1]

The basic work of the Congress, of course, is conducted through its committees and subcommittees. As discussed earlier, most of the congressional committees participate in some stage of the budgetary review process, either in the authorization or the funding of individual programs. The entire gamut of budgetary actions taken by the Congress is conducted in a fragmented fashion, even though the budget—at least the formal budget document—comes to the Congress as a unit.

---

[1] Emerson P. Schmidt, *Economic Analysis of the Budget* (Washington: Chamber of Commerce of the United States, 1963), p. 38.

The Legislation Reorganization Act of 1946 made an unsuccessful effort to improve congressional control of the budget. Section 138 of the Act created a joint committee composed of all members of the four taxation and appropriation committees of the two chambers of the Congress. It also directed that the committee (a) compare the estimated total receipts and the total expenditures proposed in the budget for the coming year, and (b) recommend a ceiling on total expenditures to serve as a control of the total amount of appropriations.

Although a noteworthy attempt, section 138 proved unworkable in the 80th and succeeding Congresses. This failure was largely attributed to the cumbersome committee setup involved and to the lack of necessary staff.[2]

Many of the more recent suggestions for changes also are in terms of establishing a new congressional committee. A joint committee on the budget or on fiscal policy has often been advocated in order to give overall consideration to revenues, appropriations, expenditures, and debt management by the Congress as a whole. It has been suggested that ranking members or representatives of the Ways and Means and Appropriations committees of the House of Representatives and the Finance and Appropriations committees of the Senate could meet as one joint committee to consider the overall aspects of the revenue and expenditure programs.

During each of the last five Congresses, the Senate has passed, frequently by unanimous consent, a bill to create a joint House-Senate Committee on the Budget (e.g., S. 537, 88th Congress). Such a committee would act as a service committee, similar to the Joint Committee on Internal Revenue Taxation on the revenue side, to aid the appropriations committees in a more systematic and detailed review of budgetary issues.[3]

Other specific legislative proposals introduced in prior Congresses to change the organization or structure of the Congress

---

[2] A more detailed discussion of the organizational aspects of congressional review of the budget will be discussed in a forthcoming AEI study by Professor John S. Saloma.

[3] U. S. Senate, Committee on Government Operations, *Create a Joint Committee on the Budget*, Hearings on S. 537, March 19 and 30, 1963; *Joint Committee on the Budget*, Senate Report No. 141, 88th Congress, 1st Session.

and of congressional units in order to improve budgetary review have included the following:

1. A joint congressional committee to audit all government agencies (Senate Joint Resolution 42, 80th Congress).

2. A Legislative Bureau of Audit and Review (Senate Bill 3482, 82d Congress).

3. A Committee on Fiscal Planning for the House of Representatives (House Resolution 481, 86th Congress).

4. A select committee to study the fiscal and budget organization and operations of the Congress.[4]

The above suggestions appear to have some merit and, if adopted, might contribute to improved congressional controls over government spending. However, either or both Houses of the Congress have consistently opposed these and similar proposals.

The proposed joint Senate-House committees generally have been turned down in the House of Representatives, which is strongly concerned with maintaining its primacy on financial matters. The constitutional mandate that all revenue bills must originate in the House has been interpreted to cover also bills to appropriate the revenues, although there may be some arguments to the contrary.[5] Attempts to establish new committees in either House also have been interpreted as being dilutions of the powers and responsibilities of the respective appropriations committee and, hence, have been unsuccessful.

It appears to the writer that future attempts to improve congressional budgetary control must take into account these fundamental jurisdictional considerations.

Congressional Procedures

Another "family" of suggested improvements covers omnibus appropriation bills, special sessions, joint hearings, and similar

---

[4] Cf. U. S. Senate Committee on Government Operations, *Financial Management in the Federal Government*, Senate Document No. 11, 87th Congress, 1st Session, pp. 221-31, 363-69.

[5] "Authority of the Senate to Originate Appropriation Bills," staff memorandum reprinted in U. S. Senate, Committee on Government Operations, *Create a Joint Committee on the Budget*, Hearings, *op. cit.*, pp. 81-114.

procedural changes. Although not involving changes in congressional committee structure, these proposals do require significant departures from either the way in which the Congress meets to consider the budget or in the nature of appropriation legislation.

For example, in 1949 the Senate adopted a resolution (Senate Report 616) requiring the incorporation of the traditionally separate appropriation measures into a one-package or omnibus appropriation bill. This obviously was an attempt to have the Congress act from a total-budget viewpoint. At the insistence of its Appropriations Committee that existing authority was adequate, the House of Representatives declined to report a bill to authorize this change.

The House Appropriations Committee did voluntarily adopt the procedure recommended by the Senate for the fiscal year 1951. However, because of dissatisfaction compounded by the additional requirements of the Korean War, the House Committee subsequently voted to return to the old procedure of reporting separate appropriation bills for the following years.

Specific objections to the omnibus measure included that of the delay caused in passage of appropriations, due to the fact that the Senate would have been prevented from starting work on the many appropriation items until all of them were approved by the House. Also, the omnibus bill lent itself to the addition of legislative riders. As a practical matter, the President could not have vetoed such riders which he deemed objectionable unless he were willing to veto the whole omnibus bill and delay (except for temporary continuing appropriations) the financing of all government agencies.

Other procedural suggestions have been for the appropriations committees of both Houses to hold joint hearings on the appropriation bills; for a regular annual budget session of the Congress to be held separately from the session on other legislative matters (Senate Bill 2846, 85th Congress), and for the Congress to stay in session until it balances the budget (Senate Joint Resolution 126, 84th Congress).

These various attempts to change congressional procedures have failed to obtain even the level of support gained by some of the proposals to establish new committees.

Suggested Mechanism to Assist in Budget Review

In the absence of reform of a more basic character—and with the thought of encouraging such reform—the writer suggests here a budget reviewing mechanism, representing an approach somewhat different from the previously reviewed proposals. It would not require changes in the organizational structure of the Congress or alterations in legislative-executive relationships. Rather, the suggestion is in terms of an analytical mechanism which can be used by the existing committees of the Congress.

The suggested mechanism, it is believed, would assist in overcoming the serious shortcoming in the congressional review of the budget that springs from lack of a workable means of reviewing an individual revenue or expenditure decision in the light of the total budget picture. It also should be helpful in the matter of alternative choices by the Congress in attacking the budget problem.

A Budgetary Scorecard. Table 15 presents the framework of this suggested tool of budgetary review. In the form of a "Budgetary Scorecard," it is intended to be a very simple, straightforward application of economic analysis to pertinent budget facts. In essence, its purpose would be to show the effect of individual budget decisions (i.e., viewing each case as the marginal case) on the overall state of federal finances.[6]

The budgetary scorecard would be far less ambitious than the earlier proposals reviewed here. It merely would be intended to serve as an informational aid to the various congressional committees that act on authorizing or appropriating legislation. It is put forward in the hope that it might constitute a small, initial step towards increasing more effective congressional control over government spending.

Except for using the 1964 budget estimates for the "submission" columns for the fiscal years 1963 and 1964, the scorecard contains hypothetical data for illustration only.

---

6 Cf. Professor Paul McCracken's statement, "Whatever the details of the solution may be, this absence of any explicit Congressional consideration of total expenditures remains in principle an important gap in budgetary procedures." "Budgetary Concepts: A Symposium," *Review of Economics and Statistics,* May 1963, p. 147.

Table 15

ILLUSTRATIVE BUDGETARY SCORECARD

(On Basis of Cash Receipts from and Payments to Public)

	1963 (Current Year) Submission	1963 (Current Year) Revision	1964 (Budget Year) Submission	1964 (Budget Year) Revision	1965 (Future Effect) Estimate	1965 (Future Effect) Revision
Budget Totals (billions of dollars):						
Receipts	$108.4	$108.0	$112.2	$112.5	$116.0	$115.0
Expenditures	116.8	116.0	122.5	124.0	125.0	128.0
Deficit (or surplus)	$—8.3	$—8.0	$—10.3	$—11.5	$—9.0	$—13.0
Item Under Consideration:						
To Extend Assistance to Schools in Federally Affected Areas (millions of dollars)						
Allowance contained in above estimates: Expenditures (NOA)	......	......	148 (254)	165 (270)	250 (260)	265 (280)
Amount being considered: Expenditures (NOA)	......	......	......	200 (300)	......	300 (350)
INCREASE (or decrease) in budget deficit	......	......	......	+35	......	+35

Several assumptions have been made in "filling out" the score-card:

(1) That some congressional committee or staff (to be discussed below) has supplied (a) the revisions for 1963 and 1964 in the light of congressional action since the original submission of the 1964 budget and (b) the data for the following year (1965, in this case), to provide some indication of the future or "full year" effect of the current congressional decisions.

(2) That the estimated deficit for the budget year (1964) has been increased through more liberal congressional action on previous items.

(3) Regarding the specific item under consideration, that pressures are evident to increase the existing program of aid to schools in areas heavily affected by federal activities because of the deferral of the President's proposal for a broad program of general aid to education.

Hopefully, the type of information in Table 15 would show the congressional committee that (1) the prospective deficit for 1964 is larger than 1963, (2) congressional action to date has increased the prospective deficit further, and (3) the specific item under consideration, if enacted at the currently recommended level, would raise the budget deficit further still.

It is problematical whether such data would, in fact, have any influence upon the deliberations of individual committees. It would, however, provide a simple technique and substantiating figures for specific members of these committees who desired analytical support for their positions.

As the scorecard might be used in conjunction with actions on a variety of expenditure authorization, appropriation, and revenue bills, it would maintain constantly for the attention of the Congress a recording of the ebb and flow of the current status of the budget picture for the ensuing fiscal year (or current year after the July 1 milestone in a congressional session). The trend of congressional actions toward a larger or smaller deficit, or a balanced budget or surplus status would be clearly revealed.

At the same time, use of the scorecard would be a means of appraising in concrete terms the effects of each individual fiscal action on the total budget outcome.

Implementation of Scorecard Procedure. Use of the score-card idea would require services of staff personnel of congressional committees or administrative agencies, to do the "book-keeping" and to develop estimates of effects on expenditure or revenue figures of individual actions changing proposed new obligational authorization or affecting anticipated revenues. Also, the device could be expanded if congressional committees dealing with substantive legislation would undertake, to a greater degree than has been the case in the past, to elicit from proponents of new expenditure programs their best estimates (with supporting data) of anticipated expenditures under the program for at least a five-year period into the future.

A number of decisions would need to be made on matters of implementation. For one thing, the initial estimates of total receipts and expenditures either could be taken directly from the presidential recommendations or could be subject to change by a congressional committee (such as by substituting the revenue estimates prepared by the staff of the Joint Committee on Internal Revenue Taxation).

Also, the choice of budget concept would have to be made, such as between the administrative budget or the statement of cash receipts from and payments to the public. Because of the more comprehensive coverage of the latter, it has been used in Table 15.[7]

As previously indicated, the current reporting of budgetary action envisioned in the proposed "scorecard" would not be limited to pending actions by the appropriations committees but would also be utilized by the substantive committees considering basic legislation. Hence, the birthstage of government spending programs, now often relatively immune from budgetary considerations, would be exposed to the type of financial concern currently shared only by the appropriations and tax-writing committees.

The scorecard would also constitute a first step attempt to extend the time horizon of federal budgeting. Estimates of fu-

---

[7] The alternative budget concepts are discussed below. For a clear and straightforward explanation of the desirability of such a comprehensive cash concept, see Chamber of Commerce of the United States, *Improving the Federal Budget*, report of a special committee established at the request of President Kennedy, 1962.

ture year expenditure impacts of new programs would not be binding but they would at least apprise the Congress of spending plans anticipated for the future.

This type of information on future impacts could be especially useful in connection with reviews of proposed new programs where the initial requirements appear to be small, but the total eventual cost may substantially exceed the value of benefits to be derived. The Senate Subcommittee on National Policy Machinery has colorfully stated that "a 12-month budget reveals only the top of the fiscal iceberg." [8]

The scorecard could be maintained by the staffs, possibly augmented, of the appropriations committees of each chamber. Alternatively, the task could be assigned to a Joint Committee on the Budget should the Congress decide to establish one. Another possibility would be to develop the capabilities of the General Accounting Office, which is a congressional rather than executive agency. The staff involved would need to keep abreast of the actions of the various substantive committees which provide financial authorization for future federal spending. Also, the working relationships would have to be developed so that the scorecards, when properly prepared and made available, would actually be utilized in the deliberations of these various committees.

During the past year, a very short "score-keeping" step has been taken through progress reports on appropriation legislation inserted by the chairman of the House Appropriations Committee in the *Congressional Record*.[9] Representative Cannon included a summary of the action which had been taken on the appropriation bills during the current congressional session, together with an approximation of the portions of the President's budget which were yet to come before the House of Representatives for consideration.

However, Mr. Cannon's summary excluded, by its very nature, the various permanent appropriations as well as "backdoor" spending authorizations which are reported by the substantive committees rather than being included in the appropriations leg-

---

[8] U. S. Senate, Committee on Government Operations, Subcommittee on National Policy Machinery, *The Bureau of the Budget and the Budgetary Process* (Washington: U. S. Government Printing Office, 1961), p. 4.

[9] Cf. June 17, 1963, pp. 10305-07.

islation. Also, the congressional report is on the basis of appropriations (including the *pro forma* appropriations to liquidate contract authorizations) rather than the more comprehensive "new obligational authority" concept used in the budget. By its very nature, Representative Cannon's report is based on the conventional budget concept, rather than the more embrasive cash approach used in Table 15.

Although a step in the right direction, Mr. Cannon's report is in the form of general background information and apparently does not yet enter into the deliberations of the various committees. The "scorecard" suggested here might overcome that hurdle if it were in the form of an official communication presented to each congressional committee whenever it was about to consider a specific item of legislation containing financial authorization.

Choice of Budget Concept

Because the amount of money expended by the Federal Government during any given period is a matter of political controversy as well as economic analysis, several different methods of measuring the level of government spending have come into use. As will be demonstrated subsequently, the selection of a budget concept may in some circumstances significantly alter conclusions concerning the Federal Government's financial activities.

The three most widely used measures of federal spending are budget expenditures, cash payments to the public, and federal expenditures on income and product account (see Figure 4).

Budget expenditures. The most widely reported of the three series, budget expenditures, are computed on the basis of the administrative, or conventional, budget. This covers generally the government funds which are or can be subject to annual executive and legislative control.

The "budget expenditures" generally include all expenditures of the federal departments and agencies, plus the net outlays of the enterprises which are wholly owned by the Federal Government. They exclude the transactions of government-sponsored enterprises and trust funds and payments for retiring, purchasing, or redeeming the government's debt. This treatment is similar to that of many business firms whose budgets usually exclude the company pension funds and the operations of firms in which they only have a partial interest.

For the government enterprises which are included, usually only the net expenditures—the difference between gross disbursements and gross receipts—are reported in the total of budget expenditures. A number of exceptions, however, exist to this "net" treatment of government enterprises. Some government agencies which are not financially organized as business-type enterprises, notably the power marketing agencies of the Department of the Interior, deposit the proceeds from their operations directly into the Treasury. In such cases, these receipts do not offset budget expenditures but increase the totals of budget receipts. Either treatment has the same effect on the budget surplus or deficit.

Through the years, the items included in the budget totals have varied considerably. The more important changes are mentioned as an indication of the possibilities for future changes and improvements.

A number of items previously included on both the income and outgo sides have been gradually excluded. Beginning in 1948, capital transfers, such as payments to the Treasury by wholly owned government corporations for retirement of capital stock, have been excluded from both budget receipts and expenditures. Starting the following year, amounts refunded by the government, principally for overpayment of taxes, have been reported as deductions from total receipts rather than as budget expenditures.

Prior to 1953, the payroll taxes collected for the railroad retirement trust fund were included as budget receipts. The transfers of these receipts to the trust fund were also included as budget expenditures. They are now netted out of budget receipts and do not appear in budget expenditures. The exclusion of these items from both the receipt and expenditure totals has no effect on the budget surplus or deficit.

Cash payments to the public. The most comprehensive of the three measures of government spending, cash payments, are computed on the basis of what has come to be called the consolidated cash budget. Essentially, this measures the total flow of cash, exclusive of borrowing and the repayment of borrowing, between the government and the public. The public in this sense includes business firms, individuals, state and local governments, foreign governments, and international agencies. Cash payments include the operations of the many trust funds of the government, such as those for social security and unemployment compensation, and the operations of government-sponsored enterprises in which the Federal Government has had a share of ownership from time to time. The latter include the Banks for Cooperatives, Federal Home Loan Banks, and Federal Deposit Insurance Corporation.

Federal expenditures on income and product account. The newest of the three measures, federal expenditures on income and product account, represents the total of all the portions of federal spending that are included in the Gross National Product or related statistics. This measure includes direct purchases from business, transfer payments to individuals, and grants-in-aid to state and local governments. It excludes such capital items as loans and purchases of land and other existing assets.

The practical importance of the differences among these series may be illustrated with reference to the federal budget for the fiscal year 1964. The Budget Message states (pages 9-10):

> In presenting the budget as the Government's financial plan for 1964, I am giving major emphasis to a consolidated cash presentation, covering not only the administrative budget but also other Federal activities . . . . This provides a much more complete picture of governmental activities and finances than the administrative budget.

Nevertheless, later in the Message, the claim is made that the total of administrative budget expenditures for all programs (except national security, space, and interest) estimated for 1964 "has been held slightly below the 1963 level" (page 15). Technically, of course, the claim is correct. However, if, in keeping with the quotation above, the comparison were made on the basis of the cash budget, the claim would not have been supported. Cash payments (excepting national security, space, and interest) were estimated to rise from the fiscal year 1963 to 1964.

The illustration cited above is hardly unique. The availability of a variety of budget series lends itself to selective utilization to prove a given point or contention. It would appear more desir-

Figure 4

THREE MEASURES OF FEDERAL GOVERNMENT SPENDING
(Fiscal Year 1962)

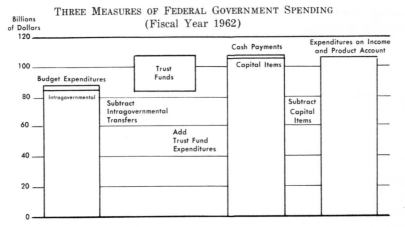

Note: Several adjustment items were too small to be charted: noncash budget expenditures (deducted to reach cash payments); government-sponsored enterprise expenditures (added to reach cash payments); miscellaneous adjustments for timing, netting and consolidation, and coverage (made in order to reach income and product expenditures).

able to have one standard measure of federal expenditures (and revenues), such as the cash budget, and to relegate other series to the subordinate status of subsidiary statements and special analyses.

This study is based on the concept of Federal Government cash payments to the public because, as demonstrated in Figure 4, it is the most comprehensive of the three available measures of government spending. Unlike the administrative budget, it includes the governmental trust funds which comprise the large and growing social security systems. Similarly, unlike the national income series, the cash payment concept includes important capital transactions such as the government lending programs.

SUMMARY AND CONCLUSIONS

PERSONS AND GROUPS concerned with budget policy—be their primary interest economy or efficiency in government operations or the use of fiscal policy to promote economic growth and stability—quickly encounter numerous legal and institutional obstacles to budgetary improvements. This study dealt with these obstacles and suggested several lines of potential improvement.

The Concentration of Pressures

Federal expenditures are very unevenly divided among the population, whether the category of analysis used is type of expenditure, location of the government activity, or the industries or groups that are benefited.

• Over 68 percent of the estimated Federal Government cash payments to the public in the fiscal year 1964 were devoted to national defense and health-labor-welfare programs.

• Over 90 percent of the contracts awarded by the Federal Government are currently being devoted to military and space programs.

• In the case of seven states—Kansas, California, Washington, New Mexico, Connecticut, Arizona, and Utah—work on defense contracts alone accounts for 20 to 30 percent of the total industrial employment.

• For individual industries, sales to the Federal Government range from 10 to 95 percent of the total.

For the individual locality, the variety of federal "largesse" which may be available, and competed for against other areas, is almost staggering. For example, 33 different federal "developmental" programs were conducted in the Atlanta metropolitan area in 1962, ranging from urban renewal and construction of roads and public buildings to saline water research and investigation of fish and wildlife.

The Mechanics of Government Spending

An examination of the entire sequence of the Federal Government spending process reveals certain key points of control, including some which are not normally regarded as part of the budget system proper.

• The enactment by the Congress of basic legislation authorizing a given government activity to be performed.

Although not a part of the formal budget process, this step comes closest to being the birth stage of government spending. In many cases, such legislation actually contains financial authorizations, bypassing the appropriations review.

• The screening of departmental budget requests by the Bureau of the Budget and the President.

• The review and approval of appropriation requests by the Congress.

The appropriation subcommittees of the Senate and House of Representatives perform the most detailed and important review. The key point of effective budgetary control by the Congress is the granting of new obligational authority, which empowers the government agencies to set in motion a chain of action that ultimately will result in a flow of expenditures.

• The apportionment of funds by the Bureau of the Budget.

The apportionment authority can be used to keep expenditures for a given activity below the level funded by the Congress.

• The payments by the Treasury.

Although this is the stage of the process on which public interest is normally focused for the control of government spending, it is the least effective of the various points of control. Generally, if a commitment has been made and costs incurred, the most that can be done at this stage is to postpone an expenditure.

Built-In Rigidities

An examination of the proposed budget for the fiscal year 1964 reveals that only 58 percent of the funds requested were subject to effective congressional review through the appropriations process. The remaining 42 percent consisted primarily of permanent indefinite appropriations, continuing construction projects, and other items relatively fixed or uncontrollable as a result of substantive legislation on the books.

• On the average, 96 percent of the budgets of the military and other national security programs for fiscal 1964 were subject to effective review. However, only 23 percent of the other agency budgets, the various domestic civilian programs, were actually subject to effective review.

• The bulk of the expenditures for the civilian, welfare agencies is authorized virtually automatically as a result of the basic, continuing commitments contained in statutes generally written by and reported out by committees of the Congress concerned with the individual program or group being benefited rather than with the state of federal finances.

• The various types of permanent budgetary commitments— such as fixed dollar amounts for certain grants to states or indefinite appropriation for given programs of the proceeds from whole categories of revenues—bear little if any relationship to the current requirements for federal expenditures. It was suggested that these commitments be reviewed in an attempt to eliminate them or at least convert them to permissive, authorizing legislation which would require annual congressional action on appropriation requests. There was a further suggestion of the desirability of an exhaustive re-examination of all basic laws creating fixed-cost obligations, with particular reference to terms and conditions under which the obligations accrue.

Proposed new expenditure programs provided for by the proposed 1964 budget were listed for the purpose of illustrating the great variety of these potential additions to the "uncontrollable area" of the budget.

The Choice Among Alternatives

It also was suggested that the budget recommendations be submitted and reviewed within a framework which would permit choices among alternatives—the conscious allocation of budget funds among the major purposes of government. Such a systematic approach is not now discernible within the budget process. An attempt to outline such an allocative framework for the 1964 budget revealed that:

• A large portion, but less than half, of the budgeted expenditures were devoted to the national security.

• The great bulk of all nondefense spending was allocated to the various welfare programs.

• About one-fifth of the funds for national security do not go directly to the U. S. Armed Forces, but are devoted to nonmilitary forms of competition or to foreign aid. (This was an example, among many, of a situation wherein the government conducts a variety of programs to achieve the same objective but does not compare directly the efficiency of the allocation of funds among these alternative means to a given end.)

The essential question to be considered is: "Would an extra dollar be more wisely spent for Program A or for Program B?" This fundamental question implicit in the allocation of budgeted funds is not raised in the overall budgetary process at present. Yet it is no more novel than a family's decision to use the Christmas bonus for a new car or a vacation, or a company's decision to use an increase in earnings to raise the dividend rate or to embark upon a new research program.

Improvements in Budget-Control Techniques

Because of renewed interest in the problems of federal expenditure control, plans that have been proposed in the past for improvements in budget reviewing techniques were reviewed. Finally, a procedure was suggested, as a step in the direction of such improvements, in the form of a "Budgetary Scorecard." The suggested scorecard is intended as a procedural means of enabling congressional committees and subcommittees, and the Congress as a whole, to focus attention on the total budget picture as actions are taken on individual bills appropriating funds or creating new expenditure programs.

APPENDIX A
GLOSSARY OF FEDERAL BUDGET TERMINOLOGY

Allotment—An authorization by the head or other authorized employee of a Federal Government agency to incur obligations within a specified amount pursuant to an appropriation or other statutory provision.

Apportionment—A distribution made by the Bureau of the Budget of amounts available for obligation or expenditure in an appropriation or fund account into amounts available for specified time periods, activities, functions, projects, or objects. The amounts so apportioned limit the obligations to be incurred or, when so specified, expenditures to be accrued.

86

Appropriation—A statutory authorization to make payments out of the Treasury for specified purposes.

Appropriation or fund account—An account established to make amounts available for obligation and expenditure from the Treasury. These accounts include not only those to which money is directly appropriated, but also revolving funds and trust funds.

A *one-year account* is one which is available for the incurring of obligations only during a specified fiscal year.

A *multiple-year account* is one which is available for the incurring of obligations for a definite period in excess of one fiscal year.

A *no-year account* is one which is available for the incurring of obligations for an indefinite period of time.

Authorization to expend from debt receipts—A statutory authorization to make payments for specified purposes out of moneys derived from the sales of securities rather than through direct appropriations (this differs from receipts from operations which are handled differently by the various agencies).

An *authorization to expend from public debt receipts* relates to moneys derived from the sale of public debt securities of the Federal Government.

An *authorization to expend from corporate debt receipts* relates to moneys derived from the sale of corporate debt securities.

Contract authorization—A statutory authorization under which contracts or other obligations may be entered into prior to an appropriation for the payment of such obligations.

Fiscal year—The period beginning July 1 and ending June 30 of the following calendar year. The fiscal year is designated by the calendar year in which it ends, e.g., the fiscal year 1964 is the year beginning July 1, 1963, and ending June 30, 1964.

Fund, trust—A fund established to account for the receipts which are held in trust for use in carrying out specific purposes and programs in accordance with an agreement or a statute.

New obligational authority—The sum of new authorizations to incur obligations. New obligational authority includes appropriations other than appropriations to liquidate contract authorizations, contract authorizations, authorizations to expend from debt receipts and authorizations which continue available any unobligated balances of these authorizations which were made for current operations of the year and which would otherwise expire for obligation purposes.

A *definite authorization* is one the amount of which is stated as a specific sum at the time the authorization is made (whether in an appropriation act or other law).

An *indefinite authorization* is one the amount of which is not stated as a specific sum when the authorization is made, but is determinable only at some future date, such as an appropriation of all or part of the receipts from a certain source.

A *permanent authorization* is one automatically made each year over a period of time by virtue of standing legislation, without annual action by Congress.

A *current authorization* is one enacted by Congress in or immediately preceding the fiscal year.

Obligations incurred—Amounts of orders placed, contracts awarded, services received, and similar transactions during a given period requiring disbursement of money. They include disbursements not preceded by the recording of obligations.

Reserves, budgetary—Portions of appropriations, funds, or contract authorizations set aside by the Bureau of the Budget for (a) savings which are made possible by or through changes in requirements, greater efficiency of operations, or other developments subsequent to the date on which the authorization was made available, and (b) contingencies.

APPENDIX B
DETAILED PROGRAM COMPOSITION OF THE
1964 BUDGET[1]

NEW OBLIGATIONAL AUTHORITY
(millions of dollars)

NATIONAL SECURITY

	Amount	Comment
U. S. Military Forces		
Department of Defense	$49,989	Covers all of the traditional military functions of the DOD except retired pay and family housing
Atomic Energy Commission....	1,446	Assumed at one-half of total AEC budget
Selective Service System	38	Military personnel acquisition
Subtotal	$51,473	

[1] In the form as first submitted in January 1963.

	Amount	Comment
U. S. Passive Defense		
Office of Emergency Planning	18	Civil defense
Department of Defense	300	Civil defense activities
Subtotal	$ 318	
Foreign Military Forces		
Military assistance	$ 1,480	Military portion of foreign aid program
Foreign Non-Military Activities		
Foreign assistance—economic	$ 4,421	All
Peace Corps	108	All
International Financial Institutions	112	U. S. contribution to Inter-American Development Bank, etc.
Department of Defense	48	Panama Canal, etc.
Subtotal	$ 4,689	
Arms Control and Disarmament		
U. S. Arms Control and Disarmament Agency	$ 15	All
Political and Psychological Competition		
U. S. Information Agency......	$ 217	All
Scientific Competition		
National Aeronautics and Space Administration	$ 5,712	All
Total, National Security..	$63,904	

PUBLIC WELFARE

	Amount	Comment
Life Insurance and Retirement Programs		
Department of Defense	$ 1,163	Retired pay
Department of Health, Education, and Welfare	16,822	Old-age, survivors and disability insurance system
Veterans Administration	758	National Service Life Insurance
Railroad Retirement Board....	1,231	Railroad Retirement System
The Judiciary	1	⎫ Government employees retirement systems
Department of State	8	⎬
Civil Service Commsson	2,331	⎭
Subtotal	$22,314	

90

	Amount	Comment
Unemployment Insurance		
Department of Labor	$ 4,407	Unemployment trust fund
Health		
Department of Health, Education, and Welfare	$ 1,861	Public Health Service, etc.
Treasury Department	5	Narcotics Bureau
Veterans Administration	1,218	Veterans' medical program
Subtotal	$ 3,084	
Public Assistance		
Department of Health, Education and Welfare	$ 3,119	Grants to states for public assistance
Veterans Administration	1,800	Pensions for veterans without service-connected disabilities
Subtotal	$ 4,919	
Veterans Compensation		
Veterans Administration	$ 2,061	Compensation for service-connected disabilities
Assistance to Farmers and Rural Areas		
Department of Agriculture	$ 7,227	Farm price supports and other subsidies
Department of the Interior	63	Shared revenues with local governments
Subtotal	$ 7,290	
Urban Housing and Facilities		
Department of Defense	$ 734	Family housing
Housing and Home Financing Agency	932	All, except urban transportation
National Capital Planning Commission	1	All
Subtotal	$ 1,667	
Miscellaneous Welfare		
Disaster Relief	$ 20	All
Transitional Grants to Alaska	3	All
Department of Defense	18	Cemeterial expenses
Department of Health, Education, and Welfare	21	Juvenile delinquency, etc.
Department of the Interior	216	Indian welfare
Department of Labor	356	Manpower training, etc.
Treasury Department	34	Aid to Puerto Rico
Veterans Administration	473	Administrative expenses
American Battle Monuments Commission	2	All
Subtotal	$ 1,143	
Total, Public Welfare	46,885	

ECONOMIC DEVELOPMENT

	Amount	Comment
Natural Resources		
Department of Agriculture....	$ 879	Forest Service and Soil Conservation
Department of Defense	1,104	Corps of Engineers
Department of the Interior	1,010	Water, power, recreation, etc.
Atomic Energy Commission....	1,447	One-half of total
TVA	44	All
Subtotal	$ 4,484	
Transportation Facilities		
Department of Commerce	$ 3,772	Mainly highways
Department of the Interior	18	Indian roads
Treasury Department	364	Coast Guard
Federal Aviation Agency	810	All
Housing and Home Finance Agency	100	Urban transportation
National Capital Transportation Agency	2	All
Subtotal	$ 5,066	
Education and General Research		
Department of Commerce	$ 148	Standards, Geological Survey, etc.
Department of Health, Education, and Welfare	2,082	Office of Education, etc.
Department of Labor	20	Economic research
National Science Foundation..	589	All
Subtotal	$ 2,839	
Economic Regulation		
Department of Agriculture	$ 1	Commodity Exchange Authority
Department of the Interior....	1	Oil and gas regulation
Department of Justice	7	Antitrust
Department of Labor	30	Wages, hours, reports, etc.
CAB	11	All (except subsidies)
FCC	17	All
Federal Maritime Commission	3	All
FPC	13	All
FTC	13	All
ICC	25	All
NLRB	23	All
Renegotiation Board	3	All
SEC	14	All
Tariff Commission	3	All
Subtotal	$ 164	
Aids and Subsidies to Businesses		
Department of Agriculture....	$ 87	Statistics, etc.
Department of Commerce	776	Maritime, etc.

	Amount	Comment
Department of the Interior......	5	Lead and zinc subsidies
Department of Labor	1	Mexican farm labor
Post Office Department............	565	Postal deficit
CAB	83	Airline subsidy
Farm Credit Administration..	3	All
Federal Mediation and Conciliation Service	6	All
National Mediation Board......	2	
Small Business Administration	215	All
Subtotal	$ 1,743	
Total, Economic Development	$14,296	

GOVERNMENT OPERATIONS

	Amount	Comment
Interest Payments		
Treasury Department	$10,103	Mainly interest on the public debt
Legislative Functions		
Legislative Branch	$ 123	All (except Government Printing Office)
Judicial and Law Enforcement		
The Judiciary	$ 69	All
Department of Justice	348	All (except anti-trust)
Treasury Department	10	Secret Service
Commission on Civil Rights....	1	All
Tax Court	2	All
Subtotal	$ 430	
Housekeeping Functions		
Executive Office of the President	$ 15	All (except OEP)
President's Emergency Fund..	1	All
Legislative Branch	27	Government Printing Office
Treasury Department	802	Tax collection, check payments, etc.
General Services Administration	659	All
Civil Service Commission	49	All
Foreign Claims Settlement Commission	50	All
GAO	47	All
Smithsonian Institution	24	All
Miscellaneous Agencies	2	All
District of Columbia	452	All
Undistributed Pay Increases..	200	All
Contingencies	250	All
Subtotal	$ 2,578	

	Amount	Comment
Conducting Foreign Relations		
Department of the Interior....	$ 36	Trust territories, etc.
Department of Labor	1	Foreign labor exchanges
Department of State	374	All
Subtotal	$ 411	
Total, Government Operations	13,645	
GRAND TOTAL	$138,730	

Source: *The Budget of the United States Government for the Fiscal year Ending June 30, 1964* (Washington: U. S. Government Printing Office, 1963), pp. 128-321.

BIBLIOGRAPHY

Edward C. Banfield. "Congress and the Budget: A Planner's Criticism," *American Political Science Review*, December 1949.

Gerhard Colm with the assistance of Marilyn Young. *The Federal Budget and the National Economy*, National Planning Association, Planning Pamphlet No. 90, March 1955.

Otto Eckstein. "Evaluation of Federal Expenditures for Water Resource Projects," in U. S. Congress, Joint Economic Committee, *Federal Expenditure Policy for Economic Growth and Stability* (Washington: U. S. Government Printing Office, 1957.)

Joseph P. Harris. "Needed Reforms in the Federal Budget System," *Public Administration Review*, Autumn 1952.

I. M. Labovitz. *Federal Revenues and Expenditures in the Several States, Averages for the Fiscal Years 1959-61* (Washington: Library of Congress, September 19, 1962).

Eva Mueller. "Public Attitudes Toward Fiscal Programs," *Quarterly Journal of Economics*, May 1963.

David Novick. "Planning Ahead in the Department of Defense," *California Management Review*, Summer 1963.

Arthur Smithies. *The Budgetary Process in the United States* (New York: McGraw-Hill Book Co., 1955).

U. S. Commission on Organization of the Executive Branch of the Government. *Budgeting and Accounting* (Washington: U. S. Government Printing Office, 1949).

U. S. President. *The Budget of the United States Government for the Fiscal Year Ending June 30, 1964* (Washington: U. S. Government Printing Office, 1963 [including Appendix]).

U. S. Senate, Committee on Government Operations. *Role of the Federal Government in Metropolitan Areas* (Washington: U. S. Government Printing Office, 1963).

Robert A. Wallace. *Congressional Control of Federal Spending* (Detroit: Wayne State University Press, 1960).

Murray L. Weidenbaum. "The Economic Impact of the Government Spending Process," *The Business Review*, The University of Houston, Spring 1961.

PUBLICATIONS

STUDIES

The Rural Electrification Administration—An Evaluation, *John D. Garwood* and *W. C. Tuthill*—1963

The Economic Analysis of Labor Union Power, Revised Edition, *Edward H. Chamberlin*—1963

United States Aid to Yugoslavia and Poland—Analysis of a Controversy, *Milorad M. Drachkovitch*—1963

Communists in Coalition Governments, *Gerhart Niemeyer*—1963

Subsidized Food Consumption, *Don Paarlberg*—1963

Automation — The Impact of Technological Change, *Yale Brozen*—1963

Essay on Apportionment and Representative Government, *Alfred de Grazia*—1963 ($2.00)

American Foreign Aid Doctrines, *Edward C. Banfield*—1963

The Rescue of the Dollar, *Wilson E. Schmidt*—1963

The Role of Gold, *Arthur Kemp*—1963

Pricing Power and "Administrative" Inflation—Concepts, Facts and Policy Implications, *Henry W. Briefs*—1962

Depreciation Reform and Capital Replacement, *William T. Hogan*—1962

The Federal Antitrust Laws, *Jerrold G. Van Cise*—1962

Consolidated Grants: A Means of Maintaining Fiscal Responsibility, *George C. S. Benson* and *Harold F. McClelland*—1961

Inflation: Its Causes and Cures, Revised and Enlarged Edition, *Gottfried Haberler*—1961

The Patchwork History of Foreign Aid, *Lorna Morley* and *Felix Morley*—1961

U. S. Immigration Policy and World Population Problems, *Virgil Salera*—1960

Voluntary Health Insurance in the United States, *Rita R. Campbell* and *W. Glenn Campbell*—1960

Unionism Reappraised: From Classical Unionism to Union Establishment, *Goetz Briefs*—1960

United States Aid and Indian Economic Development, *P. T. Bauer*—1959

Improving National Transportation Policy, *John H. Frederick*—1959

The Question of Governmental Oil Import Restrictions, *William H. Peterson*—1959

Labor Unions and the Concept of Public Service, *Roscoe Pound*—1959

Labor Unions and Public Policy, *Edward H. Chamberlin, Philip D. Bradley, Gerard D. Reilly*, and *Roscoe Pound*—1958, 177 pp. ($4.50)

National Aid to Higher Education. *George C. S. Benson* and *John M. Payne*—1958

Agricultural Surplus and Export Policy, *Raymond F. Mikesell*—1958

Post-War West German and United Kingdom Recovery, *David McCord Wright*—1957

The Regulation of Natural Gas, *James W. McKie*—1957

Legal Immunities of Labor Unions, *Roscoe Pound*—1957

*Automation—Its Impact on Economic Growth and Stability, *Almarin Phillips*—1957

*Involuntary Participation In Unionism, *Philip D. Bradley*—1956

The Role of Government in Developing Peaceful Uses of Atomic Energy, *Arthur Kemp*—1956

The Role of The Federal Government in Housing, *Paul F. Wendt*—1956

The Upper Colorado Reclamation Project, Pro by *Sen. Arthur V. Watkins*, Con by *Raymond Moley*—1956

*Federal Aid to Education—Boon or Bane? *Roger A. Freeman*—1955

States Rights and the Law of Labor Relations, *Gerard D. Reilly*—1955

Three Taft-Hartley Issues: Secondary Boycotts, "Mandatory" Injunctions, Replaced Strikers' Votes, *Theodore R. Iserman*—1955

What Price Federal Reclamation, *Raymond Moley*—1955

Private Investments Abroad, *Charles R. Carroll*—1954

Farm Price Supports—Rigid or Flexible, *Karl Brandt*—1954

*Currency Convertibility, *Gottfried Haberler*—1954

*The Control of the Location of Industry in Great Britain, *John Jewkes*—1952

The Walsh-Healey Public Contracts Act, *John V. Van Sickle*—1952

The Economics of Full Employment: An Analysis of the U.N.

Report on National and International Measures for Full Employment, *Wilhelm Röpke*—1952

Price Fixing for Foodstuffs, *Earl L. Butz*—1951

Manpower Needs and the Labor Supply, *Clarence D. Long*—1951

*An Economic Approach to Antitrust Problems, *Clare E. Griffin*—1951 ($1.00)

*Valley Authorities, *Raymond Moley*—1950

*Farm Price and Income Supports *O. B. Jesness*—1950

*Monetary Policy and Economic Prosperity: Testimony of Dr. W. W. Stewart (July 3-4, 1930) before the MacMillan Committee, with introduction by *Donald B. Woodward*—1950

Corporate Profits in Perspective, *John Linter*—1949

*Current Problems of Immigration Policy, E. P. Hutchinson—1949

Guaranteed Employment and Wage Plans. A Summary and Critique of the Latimer Report and Related Documents, *William A. Berridge* and *Cedric Wolfe*—1948

The Foreign Loan Policy of the United States, *J. B. Condliffe*—1947

*Proposals for Consideration by an International Conference on Trade and Employment—*J. B. Condliffe*—1946

The Market for Risk Capital, *Jules I. Bogen*—1946

Unless otherwise shown in listing, Studies 1953 and earlier, 50 cents each; 1954 to date, $1.00 each.

———

* Out of Print

LEGISLATIVE AND SPECIAL ANALYSES
87th Congress, Second Session, 1962

No. 1—The Proposal to Increase the National Debt Ceiling

No. 2—Reorganization Plan No. 1, of 1962, to Create a Department of Urban Affairs and Housing

No. 3—Foreign Trade: Part 1: The Operation, Administration, and Development of the Trade Agreements Program. *A Special Analysis*

No. 4—Foreign Trade: Part II: Economic Consequences of Trade Liberalization. *A Special Analysis.*

No. 5—Foreign Trade: Part III: Import Adjustments Assistance and Alternatives. *A Special Analysis.*

No. 6—Foreign Trade: Part V: The European Economic Community (Common Market). *A Special Analysis*

No. 7—Purchase of United Nations Bonds. Bill by *Sen. Sparkman*

No. 8—Foreign Trade: Part V: Proposals to Amend and Extend the Reciprocal Trade Agreements Legislation. *A Special Analysis*

No. 9 — Proposals to Provide Health Care for the Aged Under Social Security. Bills by *Sen. Anderson, et al.; Rep. King.*

No. 10—Tax Proposals Relating to Foreign Income. Bill by *Rep. Mills*

No. 11—Public Welfare Amendments of 1962. Bill by *Rep. Mills*

No. 12—The Drug Control Bills and Other Proposals to Amend the Food, Drug and Cosmetic Act. Bills by *Sen. Kefauver; Reps. Sullivan, Celler* and *Harris*

No. 13—The Proposed International Coffee Agreement. *A Special Analysis*

No. 14—The Pacific Northwest Power Preference Bills. Bills by *Sen. Anderson; Reps. Hansen* and *Pfost.*

88th Congress, First Session, 1963

No. 1—History and Powers of the House Committee on Rules. *Special Analysis*

No. 2—The Youth Employment Bill. Bills by *Sen. Humphrey; Rep. Perkins*

No. 3—Tax Proposals and the Federal Finances: Part I: Federal Expenditures. *A Special Analysis*

No. 4—Tax Proposals and the Federal Finances: Part II: The American Tax System: Background for Studying Proposals for Change. *A Special Analysis*

No. 5—Proposals to Increase the National Debt Ceiling. Bill by *Rep. Mills*

No. 6—Area Redevelopment Act Amendments of 1963. Bills by *Sen. Douglas and Others; Rep. Patman*

No. 7—Tax Proposals and the Federal Finances: Part III: Tax Issues of 1963. *A Special Analysis*

No. 8—The Higher Education Facilities Act of 1963. Bill by *Rep. Green* (Ore.)

No. 9—Tax Proposals and the Federal Finances: Part IV: The Proposed Revenue Act of 1963. *A Special Analysis*

No. 10—The Proposed Foreign Assistance Act of 1963. Bills by *Sen. Fulbright; Rep. Morgan*

No. 11—The Interest Equalization Tax Bill and the U. S. Balance-of-Payments Situation. Bill by *Rep. Mills*

No. 12—A Bill to Prohibit Futures Trading in Irish Potatoes. Bills by *Sen. Muskie; Rep. McIntire*

---

* Out of Print

88th Congress, Second Session, 1964

No. 1—Tax Proposals and the Federal Finances: Part V: Changes in the Proposed Revenue Act of 1964 Recommended by the Senate Committee on Finance

Single Copy One Dollar